4.95

the god-players

the god-players

With Questions for Discussion Groups

EARL JABAY ● ● ● ● ● ● ● ● ● ● ●

ZONDERVAN PUBLISHING HOUSE
OF THE ZONDERVAN CORPORATION
GRAND RAPIDS, MICHIGAN 49506

the god-players

Copyright © 1969, 1970 by Earl Jabay

Pyranee Books are published by Zondervan
Publishing House, 1415 Lake Drive, S.E.,
Grand Rapids, Michigan 49506

ISBN 0-310-26541-X

Library of Congress Catalog card number: 69-11637

Printed in the United States of America

    84   85   86   87   88 — 20   19

To my Lord—God

Preface

Never in the history of the race has man been so busily occupied with the study of himself as he is today. The behavioral scientists and religionists are turning out tons of material for us to read as we search for new knowledge about ourselves. Most of us are surprisingly eager to do our assigned reading because, quite frankly, we are enthralled and fascinated with our subject. We are unreservedly devoted to this baffling, unmanageable creature called man. No one interests us more than ourselves.

One large reason for this is that we are all egoists at heart.

And that's a problem, the world's biggest.

God has shown us how this problem is solved. God is Himself the solution.

When that fact gets through to us, we become excited about God. In fact, like Spinoza, we become a little intoxicated with Him.

So we will need to talk about God . . . and man the god-player who, as we will see, acts out his tragic role in such a way that the play often slips off into unabashed comedy. We will feel as we do when we see a person intoxicated with alcohol—should we weep over his enslaved life or may we laugh at his comical behavior? Perhaps both, and in that order, but let us not enjoy the comedy until we have seen that inwardly shackled person set free by God.

The *way* to inner freedom is the very Way which so excited the early Christians. Today we have a great deal of difficulty understanding and entering into Christ's Way largely, I feel, because our habits of thinking, as formed by subtle cultural and philosophical influences, form a barrier to the mind-set of Christ. I have attempted in *the god-players* to capture the style of thinking which Christ and the apostles employed. It is taken for granted that the Biblical authors had their hands on the essential issues for all time and that God gave them an enlightened perspective as well as an abiding solution to human problems. I am continually trying to capture that perspective throughout these pages. At those points where we fleetingly hold it, we will either be glad because we have found the Truth that shall make us free, or we will turn away in anger, offended because our cherished ideas and attitudes are challenged.

Before we begin, however, a few practical matters.

My thanks to Dr. Louis Benes for permission to incorporate in this book a few of my articles already published in the *Church Herald*.

Alan Hagenbuch made many helpful and wise suggestions in the preparation of the manuscript.

I am also indebted to Allen G., a member of Alcoholics Anonymous, who gave permission to incorporate in the Appendix the unforgettable and highly instructive story of his life.

Princeton, N.J.   EARL JABAY

Contents

PART I
WHO IS MAN?

1. Man Is Human Spirit 13
2. God's Astonishing Appraisal 18

PART II
MAN'S PREPOSTEROUS MADNESS

3. The Self-Enthroned Egoist 27
4. The Ultimatized Man 40
5. Living Against People 50
6. Playing God 62
7. Law and License 72
8. The Action of Guilt 80
9. The Life of Bondage 84

PART III
LIFE THROUGH DEATH

10. The Way of the Cross 95
11. The Death of Our Freedom 101
12. The Death of Our Egoism 109
13. The Death of Our Guilt 115

10 • contents

14. The Death of Loneliness 122

15. The Life Which Is Really Living 128

A. "In the Middle, Einstein"—by Allen G. 139

B. The Twelve Steps—by Alcoholics Anonymous . . . 148

C. Private Confession in the Cure of Souls—by John Calvin 150

D. Questions for Discussion 152

Scripture Index 157

Subject Index 159

PART I
Who Is Man?

1. Man is human spirit

One of the first things the Scriptures tell us about man is that he bears a likeness to God. "So God created man in his own image"; then the account repeats for emphasis "in the image of God he created him"; and to make it absolutely clear to us, it is added, "male and female he created them" (Genesis 1:27).

That statement that we are created in the image of God has always intrigued me but its meaning was never quite clear. I remember that when I was a young catechumen I asked my pastor for an explanation. He pointed me to the words of the Heidelberg Catechism where it states that "God created man good, and after His own image; that is, in true righteousness and holiness, that he might rightly know God his Creator, heartily love Him, and live with Him in eternal blessedness to praise and glorify Him." That these were good words, I still have no doubt, but they did not clarify for me what was meant by the image of God in man.

Since the days of my catechetical instruction, I have spent more than a score of years reading particularly the Reformed theologians on this matter but without finding a satisfactory explanation. It may be that the theologians have somewhere adequately explained the *imago dei,* but either I could not find the explanation, or, having found it, I was not ready to understand its meaning. Looking back, I suspect that the latter possibility may indeed have been the case for one does not really understand until there is a readiness to receive.

At any rate, a few years ago, while meditating on this puzzling phrase, it finally occurred to me to take the words "in the image of God" in their simplest sense. That is, as God is Spirit, so man is spirit. Man is essentially a spiritual being, related to and of a type similar to God the Eternal Spirit. Human spirit and Divine Spirit are not the same but they are in the same spiritual order. Man, being created, is lower in the spiritual order than God, for "thou

13

hast made him little less than God," but man is highly honored in that "Thou hast given him dominion over the works of thy hands" (Psalm 8:5, 6).

That *man is human spirit* is a profound and difficult thought. It means that an unimaginable gift has come to us, in that we are in the same spiritual order as God. It means that we are not what we externally appear to be. It also means that man is quite as indefinable and as descriptively elusive as God Himself. The most the word *spirit* can do is tell us that what we really are cannot be seen. The word covers our ignorance of man—that invisible inhabitor of the spirit world. The spirit itself cannot be known, only the results of its action.

Would it not be wise, then, to leave the idea of man as a human spirit in the dusty tomes of forgotten theologians? Of what possible use is this concept? In a moment we will struggle with these questions, but first let us observe that two world-famous psychiatrists make the *imago dei* the point of departure in their thought-systems as well as in their treatment programs. Dr. Viktor Frankl bases his system of logotherapy on the simple yet profound assumption that man *is* a spirit but *has* a body. "In the logotherapeutic theory of man, it is the spiritual dimension which is of central importance. It is the spiritual which truly constitutes the person. While it is proper to say that one *has* a psyche, or a body, he must say that he *is* a spiritual being."[1]

Another religiously oriented psychiatrist, Dr. Paul Tournier, sees man as a spiritual being at the deepest level and designates that indefinable being as a person. "It is neither the body which controls the mind, nor the mind which controls the body; rather are both at once the expression of an invisible reality of a spiritual order—the person."[2] I mention these two men so that we may recognize the modern appeal of the *imago dei* concept and its relevance to human problems.

The first thing we should notice about man in the image of God is this: if man is essentially spirit then he is not essentially his feelings. To paraphrase Dr. Frankl, we may say that man *is* spirit but *has* feelings. This is something of which most of us are totally unaware. People believe that they *are* their feelings and that this is all there is to being a person. The particular manner in which we commonly describe how we feel gives evidence of our identifica-

---

[1] Donald F. Tweedie, *Logotherapy and the Christian Faith,* Grand Rapids: Baker Book House, 1961, p. 56.

[2] Paul Tournier, *The Meaning of Persons,* New York: Harper & Row, Inc., 1957, p. 104.

tion of who we are with what we feel. For we say such things as, "I am depressed," "I'm an alcoholic," "I am madly in love," all of which are literally untrue. What we really mean is that I as a human spirit am in a state of depression, or alcoholism or love.

It is a rare individual, however, who distinguishes between his spirit and his feeling-state. They are run together, unfortunately, with the disastrous result that one's spirit is obliterated by his feelings. In such a case, one lives under the tyranny of feelings. It is to this that A. A. Schneiders alludes in *The Anarchy of Feeling*[3] wherein he is critical of the "modern enthronement of feeling." He is convinced, and I agree, that the rule of feeling in human life leads inevitably to anarchy within the individual and to a destructive, sensate culture in human society.

Submission of one's spirit to the tyranny of feelings, however, is something we choose to do. We are not under a determinism which impels us to such a decision. Of course, when the human spirit capitulates to his feelings, he is then under a determinism which operates according to its own inexorable laws. Sigmund Freud and his followers have brilliantly described the path of human emotionality and conduct once it surrenders to such a determinism.

We can choose, therefore, to submit to the tyranny—I think that is the correct word to use, because our feelings can kick us around mercilessly—of our feelings, or, we can *transcend* our feeling-states by the action of our spirits. In such an act, we choose the direct opposite of what messages our feelings give us.

The best example of this is the heroic act. Lawrence Elliott in his book, *A Little Girl's Gift*[4] tells the tragic story of an eight-year old girl, Janis Babson, who contracted leukemia. Just a few hours before she died, Janis rallied enough to ask her father if he had remembered his promise to arrange to give her eyes to the Eye Bank. Mr. Babson had forgotten. Janis urgently requested that he fulfill his promise. In a short time it was arranged and soon thereafter, she bravely slipped away.

All the feelings for survival and self-preservation were pressing upon the spirit of this brave little girl. And yet, transcending all such powerful urges, not to mention her understandable burden of fear, she chose to selflessly arrange that her eyes be given to someone else through the Eye Bank. It was a heroic, altruistic act in which we search in vain for feelings of self-concern or for any prior conditioning which would account for her totally unique

---

[3] Schneiders, New York: Sheed and Ward, 1963.
[4] Elliott, New York: Holt, Rhinehart and Winston, 1963.

response to unencountered circumstances. She transcended her feeling-state with a freedom which only spiritual beings know.

No feeling need act deterministically upon the human spirit. Not even the inevitable approach of death can bind the human spirit's freedom to choose, for as Viktor Frankl has pointed out, one can always choose to use his last freedom—the choice of the manner in which one goes into death. The human spirit, admittedly, cannot transcend *any* circumstance. Surely Janis Babson could not transcend her death. But she did transcend the feelings attendant to that circumstance by the action of her human spirit, sustained as she surely was by the Holy Spirit. Janis passed on knowing the victory of her spirit's will over her emotions.

Catherine Marshall, a deeply spiritual woman, speaks of her experience with emotion and will. "Our emotions are not the real us. The motivating force at the center of our physical being is our will. The dictionary describes *will* as 'the power of conscious deliberate action.' The will is the governing power in us, the rudder, the spring of all our actions."[5] The *will* of which Mrs. Marshall speaks is roughly parallel to the undetermined choosing which is the most outstanding function of the human spirit. It is in this phenomenon of choosing that man most clearly reveals he is made in the image of God, for choosing is surely the most prominent function of the Divine Spirit.

Catherine Marshall draws a clear line between the feelings and "the real us." I think this is such an important and helpful insight. To realize that I am not my feelings is to realize that I am not an animal but a relative of God. Animals *are* their feelings. Man is not his feelings. He is a human spirit, utilizing the full range of his wonderful, God-given feelings, but always ordering them according to the will of the spirit. Mrs. Marshall correctly points out "that the Christian life must be lived in the will, not in the emotions; that God regards the decisions and choices of a man's will as the decisions and choices of man himself—no matter how contrary his emotions may be. Moreover, when this principle is applied, the emotions must always capitulate to the will."[6]

There is one more point on this matter of the *imago dei* which bears on our present study. The Bible sees man as a spiritual relative of God. Yet they are different. Man is human spirit and God is Divine Spirit. Actually, man has never had much trouble recognizing this difference. He has never seriously ever wanted to

---

[5] Catherine Marshall, *Beyond Ourselves,* New York: McGraw-Hill, 1961, p. 58.
[6] *Ibid.,* p. 56.

be anybody but man. What he does want is to be in the *position* of the Divine Spirit. Ever since the Fall, man has schemed, plotted, connived and even murdered (the Son of God) in his attempt to be positioned in a place which rightfully belongs only to the Ultimate Spirit. The long tale of Biblical history is the sad story of human spirits who, rejecting their ordained place and station in the world, made a mad attempt to wrench authority from the hands of the Almighty and then sit upon His throne. Man is free to do even that.

So the very freedom which is such a basic part of God's image in man, gives us great trouble. We feel honored by it. We are grateful for it. But we have used our freedom of choice against the Almighty.

In summary, man is a near relative of the Divine Spirit. The unique and wonderful thing about our life in the spirit world is that we can make *free* choices. I hasten to add that our choosing is surely influenced (but not determined) by our environment and that most people default in the use of their freedom by choosing to live under the tyranny of their feelings.

There is one choice, a tragic one, which all human spirits make with reference to the Divine Spirit—the decision to usurp His position of ultimate authority. As human spirits we can do that. And God, respecting our freedom, will defer to us. We are able to make ourselves "ultimate" in our world-and-life-view. To be sure, this is not man's appraisal of how we act, but it surely is the thrust of God's revelation to us. The accuracy of this appraisal can be verified in human experience, as we now hope to see.

2. God's astonishing appraisal

Perhaps the most basic choice a person makes is the way he chooses to see himself. Almost invariably, we see ourselves as though through the wrong end of a telescope. Our introspective eyes, seeing only what we want them to see, create a self-portrait in which we appear to be immature, small, innocent, victimized, too hindered by overwhelming circumstances to act much differently and too lacking in an awareness of our freedom to bear responsibility. That is, our self-image is almost always a flattering miniature of what we are in reality. You notice I hedge a little on these generalizations. That is to leave room for those exceptional instances where we truthfully appraise ourselves to be playing god. But more of that later.

The tendency to see ourselves in miniature begins early in childhood. Let us imagine a home in which a five-year old boy is standing by the crib of his newly arrived sister. The little fellow is very jealous of this new intruder. Suddenly, the boy strikes the baby. Mother sees him do it, however, and shouts: "Johnny! No! You may not hit the new baby!"

What kind of responses might we hear from Johnny?

(1) He might say: "I'm not going to talk to you anymore!" in which case he would feel he has a moral right to be resentful in the presence of his "attacking" mother.

(2) Another response might be: "Can I help it?" Here he would feel victimized by adverse circumstances. He would also feel worthy of being excused.

(3) Or, Johnny might say: "You never told me that it was naughty!" Now he accuses mother of depriving him of proper care and supervision.

(4) "I did not do it! I would *never* do a thing like that!" is another possible response. Johnny is using flat denial here and feeling very self-righteous in the face of a false accusation.

(5) Or, Johnny might cry. He would then see himself as an object of pity.

Observe that in all these illustrations, Johnny regards himself as a poor, small, little creature who feels like an abandoned orphan dumped into a cruel world. His sense of smallness causes him to defend himself with all his might. But there is another side to Johnny. It is hidden to Johnny but we can sense it. As we see Johnny in the next three responses, he sounds like a little god.

(6) "You did not see me do it!" Here he appoints himself as a judge over his mother.

(7) "I hate the baby and I hate you too!" Johnny does not hesitate to turn his wrath against mother, thereby creating a new "law" which sanctions his hatred. He feels justified in hating mother.

(8) "Oh, I hate you so much I am going to kick you!" And with this, Johnny solemnly issues himself a license to retaliate.

Were we to advise Johnny that mother *did* see him, that he has no ground for his resentment and that mother is deserving of his love and respect, he would deny it and become angry with us. He wants none of this talk about how he is in error. We see this adorable little fellow as trying to live *over* parental law and insistent upon having his own way. Johnny, however, would deny this, were we to share our feelings with him. He does not see himself in the role of Superman. Little Orphan Annie, however, would have great appeal to him because so long as Johnny can convince himself that he is a poor little orphan who is worthy of pity, he will never need to deal with his unconscious superman image.

We may observe, parenthetically, that there is a close relationship between the miniature and grandiose views of ourselves. Both views are opposite sides of the same coin. Where we find one, we find the other, and always to the same degree of distortedness in a person. Our distortedness, of course, is unconscious to us but this does not prevent us from living with a decided preference for the miniature view as our basic foundation in life. The miniature view (a) gives us a feeling of being right, (b) merely encourages us to grow a little more and (c) keeps us from making any difficult changes. The grandiose, godlike view of ourselves, on the other hand, is quite intolerable when we are conscious of it because (a) we feel guilty about it, (b) we sense that our god-ishness should go and (c) that painful changes are in order. Later, we hope to see that until the "intolerable" grandiose view is discerned and then abandoned, the miniature view will remain unchanged.

So far we have talked about the child, Johnny, but the very

attitudes we found in him are also in us adults. Come into my study and listen to a tape-recorded[1] conversation with Bob, a very gifted, middle-aged executive. If you listen closely you will hear a Johnny in Bob.

Verbatim	*Comment*
HE: And another thing I wanted to talk about was my father. I dislike my father very much. I only send him a Christmas card each year.	
I: That's all?	
HE: That's enough!	
I: Enough?	
HE: I hate him.	
I: What has he *done* to you, Bob?	
HE: Nothing—not to me nor for me.	*Bob feels a moral right to be resentful. See (1) above.*
I: Yet he is your father. He fathered you. You would not be here without your father.	
HE: My birth was the result of his accident.	*He means he was an unwanted child. He entered the world victimized by an accident and deprived of love. See (2) above.*
I: Well, a happy one for you!	
HE: Well, I have not felt that way.	
I: I know.	

[1] All recorded conversations are used with permission. The personal references are changed but not the essential content.

In this recording, the author plays the "devil's advocate" in an effort to discern and oppose the parishioner's grandiose imagery. This appraisal eventually got through to the parishioner. Dramatic changes occurred. The account of Bob is continued on page 107 ff.

HE: It is on my mind a lot. Especially at Christmas time. Christmas back home was nothing. With my wife, it is everything. But I resent the Christmases I spent with father. I hate the memory.

More feeling of having been deprived. See (3) above.

I: Christmas is a couple weeks. The rest of the time your parents cared for you when you were helpless. They changed your diapers and fed you as a baby. They gave you good training.

HE: They did *not* give me good training nor care for me.

More feeling of deprivation. See (3) above.

I: They kicked you out?

HE: I left because it was so miserable. I *still* resent my father.

Self-righteous Bob feels his leaving was justifiable. See (4) above.

I: I can't find out why.

HE: He spanked me!

An object of pity. See (5) above.

I: I spanked my kids!

HE: I am confused. My father was not good in my mother's eyes. Maybe her harangue of him seeped into me. Mother is dead. Since then my father got religion. He lived like a hellion and now that he is 70, he is getting holy.

The self-appointed Judge. See (6) above.

I: Wonderful!

HE: I think he knows he is going to die and he wants to go to heaven.

I: Anything wrong with that? Why not be thankful that he finally changed?

HE: (later) When my father came to my home, I sent him away.

Bob retaliates. See (8) above.

I: (with surprise) He came to see you? My goodness, the man *still* loves you. You send him a 10-cent Christmas card but he comes to see you!

HE: But he still calls me "Junior" when he comes!

Bob feels he has a perfect right to resent his father. See (7) above.

I: You are his son. Junior is only a name— not a judgment of your character.

In these two illustrations of Johnny and Bob, we have described how we characteristically see ourselves in miniature. Such a view might be called the natural view of man. We come by it naïvely. Once gotten, it is comfortable and easy to keep throughout life. If space would permit, we could trace how this miniature view of man is given wide application in modern, behavioral science, and no less in the various branches of Christian theology. The image of man as a struggling, basically righteous, evolving, learning and laudable individual is very precious to the human heart.

But God has contradicted the human heart.

God's revelation to us is that our view of man as someone small and innocent is fundamentally wrong. Man is not innocent. He is not basically right, humble, merely learning and co-operative—to use a few of the words we use to defend ourselves from such words as guilt, being wrong, acting arrogantly, being spoiled, being unteachable and acting obstinately.

The Word of God to us is that we have such a haughty image of ourselves, we seek even to dethrone the Almighty. Such rebellion is called sin.

When we think of a man as a sinner, therefore, let us not think of him as one to be pitied because of his frailty and moral stumblings. A sinner is a contender against God's throne. A sinner is incarnate arrogance. He is adamantly resolute that *his* will be done. Sinners are people who play god.

Scan the Scriptures and we will see an abundance of examples. Adam broke the covenant with God in the hope of becoming "as God." The Tower of Babel was a monument to human pride. The Jews in the Wilderness of Zin were constantly murmuring against God. They were "stiff-necked" and Jewish history until Christ records the sad results of their defiant godlessness. Idolatry and adultery were the big problems in Old Testament days. Idolatry was a slap in the face of the Almighty. Adultery was the epitome of man acting as a law unto himself. God's laws were ignored and in the Seventh Century, b.c., even forgotten.

In the New Testament period John the Baptist and our Lord both begin their messages with a call to repentance. "Repent—that is, think differently; change your mind, regretting your sins and changing your conduct—for the kingdom of heaven is at hand" (Matthew 3:2; see also 4:17, *The Amplified Bible*). It was an urgent call to each listener to turn away from building the kingdom of Self to a kingdom in which God is truly Lord. Listen also to Paul in his letter to the Romans: "men by their wickedness suppress the truth.... Therefore they are without excuse; for although they knew God, they did not honor him as God ... they became futile in their thinking. . . . Claiming to be wise, they became fools . . . they worshiped and served the creature rather than the Creator. . . . They were filled with all manner of wickedness . . . haters of God, insolent, haughty, boastful, inventors of evil, disobedient to parents. . . . Therefore you have no excuse, O man . . . the judgment of God rightly falls upon those who do such things. . . . But by your hard and impenitent heart you are storing up wrath for yourself on the day of wrath when God's righteous judgment will be revealed" (Romans 1:18-2:5).

God has revealed that we are not the pitiably deprived innocents we imagine ourselves to be but are rather arrogant rebels who have misused their gifts.

God has revealed to us that we have no ground for justifiable resentment, but rather that we are in the error of our stubborn ways.

God has revealed that we are unrighteous because of our ingrained egoism. He does not see us as naïve, struggling infants who are too undeveloped to bear responsibility. God calls us to account.

God has revealed that He does not excuse our sins because we are so irresistibly lovable to the Almighty. We are under the wrath of God.

God has revealed that He does not merely pity us. He judges us and then reveals a way to escape from judgment.

God contradicts the miniature view of man.

Not until a person chooses to accept the truth about his prideful self-image—that is, not until he realizes he is a sinner—is there any possibility for genuine spiritual life in that person.

Why?

For a simple, profound reason. In order to live, one must *first* die. The miniature view of man cries out to live and to grow, but a person cannot grow until he dies. Man viewed in miniature cannot enter death because the grandiose self-image must first be deeply experienced before any death can take place. The godlike self-image must first be painfully seen and then painfully die before God will construct a new life for that person.

In other words, the natural view of man (as embryonic) can issue only in death and more death (eternal death). There is no hope for life in the natural man because life comes only through death. Man, however, sees nothing about himself which is death-worthy. So he lives out his "life" which is nothing but a constant death.

If only the right thing can be crucified—the egoistic self-image—then a person can come to life. Paul speaks of this in Romans 6:6, 7: "Let us never forget that our old selves died with him on the cross that the tyranny of sin over us might be broken—for a dead man can safely be said to be immune to the power of sin. And if we were dead men with him we can believe that we shall also be men newly alive with him" (Phillips). But again, one must be aware of his egoistic self-image before it can be crucified.

This principle—that we live by dying—will be examined more in detail later. Right now, we should look more closely at the problem of egoism, for this is the central problem. Let us examine carefully the insane attempts at ego-enthronement in specific individuals and also the results of this folly upon us.

PART II
Man's Preposterous Madness

3. The self-enthroned egoist

The image of ourselves which we hold most dear is a picture of the self in miniature, as though we saw ourselves through the wrong end of a telescope. We view ourselves as puny and paltry. This is a defensive maneuver calculated to keep us from making any changes in ourselves. All that is expected of an embryo is that it will grow. We do not expect it to diminish itself or alter its defects. In the case of man, we saw that the Scriptures do not buy a simple "grow up" theory. The Bible sees man as afflicted with a grandiose egoism which must not only be diminished but die.

We are incapable, however, of seeing this in ourselves. We are, frankly, too dishonest. Thank God, however, that others who love us and wish to help us, can see how we are thinking. They frequently spot our grandiosity and at times tell us. They tell us the truth about our thinking and in this they confirm and support the Word of God which unfailingly perceives our vanity and pride. It usually takes us a long time to accept this fact—that others can see us better than we can see ourselves, but it is true. Robert Burns gives this thought classic statement when he says:

> Oh wad some Power the giftie gie us
> To see oursels as ithers see us!
> It wad frae monie a blunder free us,
> An' foolish notion.[1]

Others, therefore, must examine and describe our hearts if the true state of affairs is to be known. The truth about us is unconscious to us. Here is a task which a trusted, a wise, reliable confidant (or a confidential group) must do for us.[2] The shape of

---

[1] Burns, "To a Louse," Stanza 8.

[2] In many cases the Holy Spirit will use the Holy Scriptures themselves to help a person discern himself truthfully. A Gideon (a distribu-

our egocentricity is visible only to the eye of him who beholds us. This would certainly hold true when we think of God as the Beholder. What He sees might be described somewhat along the following lines.

In the center of every human heart is a throne. It is always occupied. Not a person in all the world is without both throne and someone occupying that throne at all times.

The aspirants to the throne are only two: God and the self—or, as we will call it, the prideful, self-centered ego. If God is enthroned by a human spirit, then that man is under the regime of the kingdom of God.[3] Man, because he is human spirit with that godlike freedom of choice, can choose who will sit on that throne. If God is enthroned, the prideful ego is dethroned and the human spirit is correctly positioned *under* God and *with* people. But when the ego is self-enthroned, God is ignored while man, who is now mispositioned in his world, plays god. It is this mispositioning of man which brings him now to live *without* God and *against* his fellow men. The tragic result of egoistic self-enthronement is correctly termed *godlessness*.

Let us try to visualize with a diagram this state of godlessness in the world of the self-enthroned egoist. Understand that this diagram is not as he sees himself, for his egoistic pride is unconscious to him. This is an attempt to state how the natural man is seen by revelation: "For the word of God is living and active, sharper than any two-edged sword, piercing to the division of soul and spirit, of joints and marrow, and discerning the thoughts and intentions of the heart. And before him no creature is hidden, but all are open and laid bare to the eyes of him with whom we have to do" (Hebrews 4:12, 13).

Here, then, is the world as created by the self-enthroned egoist.

---

tor of Bibles) told me of a man who had embezzled some funds from a bank. He left town with the money. That night he stayed in a motel in which the Gideons had placed a Bible. The man began to read and soon came to such an acute realization of his colossal arrogance and greed that it drove him to his knees in repentance. When he arose, he was a new man in Christ. To bring about a conviction of sin, God uses the witness of people who lived in Biblical times just as well as the experience of modern Christians.

[3] Think of this reign as existing inside the person, i.e., in his thoughts and world view. Jesus located His reign within the human heart when He said: "The kingdom of God never comes by watching for it. Men cannot say, 'Look, here it is,' or 'There it is,' for the kingdom of God is inside you" (Luke 17:21, Phillips).

THE WORLD OF A MISPOSITIONED PERSON

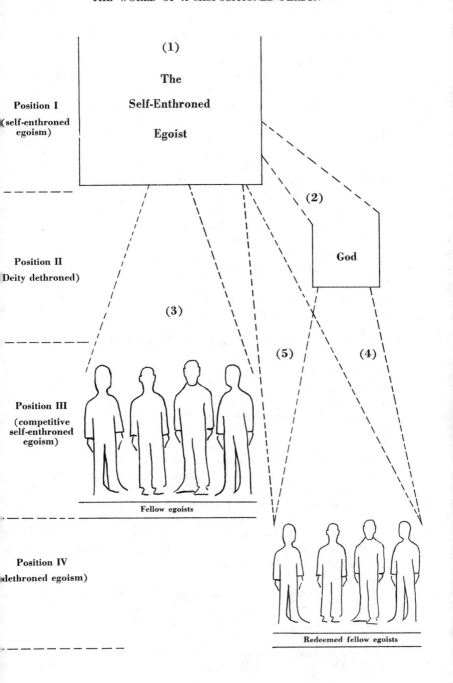

Please notice the following with regard to the diagram:

(1) The enthroned egoist positions the persons in his world at different levels. The highest, ultimate position is for himself. This places the egoist over God and fellow man.

(2) I wanted the diagram to indicate the attribute of infinity (particularly of power and knowledge) in the egoist and God. To do this, their diagrammatic representations are left open-ended. The egoist, though he knows he is not infinite, positions himself as infinite power, authority and goodness. Notice that God is thought of as divine, even infinite, but is never positioned over the egoist. So God is a divine underling in the egoist's world. God has a name but no power or authority. In this position, God is known but ignored because He has been stripped of all power.

(3) The egoist in Position I strives to live over his fellow self-enthroned egoists in Position III. It makes no sense to be on a throne if everyone else is also on it. So at best, this position leads to a highly competitive style of life, at worst to living in hostile opposition to others. Yet, because of a shared ideology, there is never total estrangement.

(4) Dethroned egoists in Position IV live under God, under Highest Power. As such they fulfill the whole duty of man—to "fear God, and keep his commandments" (Ecclesiastes 12:13).

(5) The enthroned egoist lives in opposition to the dethroned egoists just as he does with his fellow enthroned egoists. Added to this, however, is an out-of-touchness with the dethroned egoists. The enthroned egoist ignores them for the most part or, if thrown into contact, he quite literally looks down on them on two counts: (a) they have submitted to higher authority and (b) they live with (that is, noncompetitively with), their fellow men.

In order for us to better understand the problem of the mis-positioned man, I suggest we turn to page 32 and observe the two-level world of a correctly positioned, dethroned egoist.

What would be most helpful now, I feel, is to offer a few examples of mispositioning. Each is an illustration of how a person makes himself ultimate by enthroning his ego. He makes himself number one in his world because he recognizes no power or authority over himself.

A person reveals that he is under no power and authority (other than his own) when he refuses to subject himself to the authority of God which is represented to us by people, institutions and laws. There is authority vested in institutions (a nation, a business, a church, a hospital); in people whose wisdom carries authority (older people, elders in a church, the pastor who transmits sacred wisdom, a wife, a husband); in people who, by their superior knowledge, can "speak with authority" (a scientist, professor, etc.); and in laws (the Ten Commandments, traffic laws, etc.). All this authority finds its source in God, " . . . For there is no authority except from God. . . . " (Romans 13:1).

Our first example of egoistic self-enthronement is a man, let us call him Vic, who related to me some events on a certain Sunday afternoon in his life.

Around midafternoon, Vic and his wife were preparing to receive an older couple whom they had invited to their home. Vic was tense, edgy, because the guests were wealthy, prominent people whom Vic scarcely knew. He was especially irritable with his children who were asked to assist in small ways with the preparation. The tension mounted until, in an eruption of anger, Vic exploded at the children, sending them to their rooms because they were not doing their work to suit him. He proceeded to do the work himself, feeling sure that this was the only way to get things done right.

Later in the evening, the guests were in the mood for a game of Scrabble.[4] Vic had always thought of himself as a rather sharp Scrabble-player, so it was with some displeasure for Vic when the players challenged him on a word. A rule in Scrabble is that only recognized English words be used. In this instance, Vic argued that *er* was a word. A reliable dictionary was consulted and it showed Vic to be in error. That might end the matter for some people but not for our host! He insisted that the dictionary was wrong and to this day, Vic believes that somewhere in the world is a dictionary which will support him. When finally the guests had left, Vic turned to his wife and said: "I've had it! *Never* again will we have *those* people at our home!"

After Vic had finished relating this unhappy experience, I commented that he sounded rather godlike to me. His nervousness in the afternoon was caused by feeling that everything depended on him, if the evening was to be successful. Also, when the children were dismissed, this left him as the one who alone could do things right. With regard to the Scrabble game, Vic could never be wrong. And finally, in that remark after the guests left, Vic sat as judge over his guest, invoking a punitive retribution upon them. "All that sounds to me," I said, "as though you felt very godlike."

---

[4] Scrabble® is a game, usually for four people, in which letters are placed on a board to make words. Players must use one or more letters of words already on the board to form their new words. Each letter has a numerical value and the player with the highest score wins.

THE WORLD OF A POSITIONED PERSON

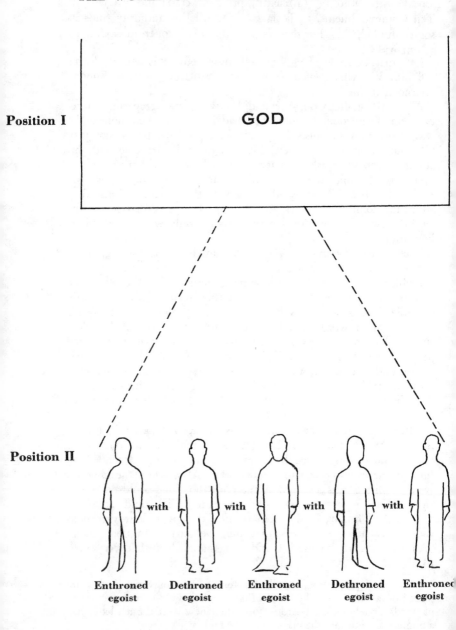

My remark rocked Vic, but at my mention of God, he managed to say: "I'd better be honest with you, pastor, I don't have much religion in me. In fact, I would rather not even talk about the Man upstairs."

As Vic spoke, I sensed a note of tragedy and embarrassment in his words. I also felt saddened because we were both looking at the same picture—an enthroned egoist who was living so competitively with God that it was painful even to speak His name. There is a reason why we speak of God as "The Big Boss," "Pop," "Someone up there," "The Man upstairs," etc. It is because our egoistic tendencies have made God into an antagonist whose very name we abhor.

Let us now look at another example—an enthroned egoist who positioned herself directly under the authority of God at the suggestion of her pastor.

Mary Temple made a frantic phone call to me one evening concerning her 12-year-old son. The boy was not doing well in school because of certain emotional problems. In addition, the impending divorce from her husband would soon break up her home and it was undecided who would have custody of the boy. This poor woman was in tears as she cried:

"What is going to happen to my boy?"

"We just don't know, Mary," I replied, regretting that my remark was so inane. I prayed silently for something better to say.

"I am worried sick," she went on. "Oh, God, there must be something I can do for the boy!"

Suddenly I found my prayer answered, for Mary had given me a cue. I knew now what to say.

"Give up your boy to God and let Him worry about your son. I urge you to give God control of the boy's life. Trust Him, Mary. Give up the claim that it all depends upon what you do."

Somehow God managed to use my stammering words but not immediately. A few days later the crisis in her life became more intense. In that private hell in which she was playing god (by worrying about a future quite out of her control), the Holy Spirit directed her to begin reading the Psalms. She had a profound religious experience as she read all 150 of them at one sitting!

When she arose, she was a dethroned person! God had become the Power-Center and the King of her life. It made no sense to worry about her boy now because the power and the direction of her life were in God's hands. She stepped down from the throne of her life and enthroned God as her Leader, Protector and King. Mary Temple stopped competing with the Almighty and gave up her presumptuous claim that she could control her future world.

This was now God's task and by His grace, Mary was able to relinquish a task which was never intended for her.

Our third illustration of self-enthroned egoism is a hospitalized alcoholic parishioner. Listen to our conversation.

HE: I'm here to learn why I am an alcoholic and how I can stop. So far, you are not getting through to me, Chaplain. You *can't* get through because you are not an alcoholic.

I: That sounds like you have built a wall between us.

HE: Since you are not an alcoholic, there is a gap between actual field experience and theory. I know mental anguish from experience. You read about it.

I: Obviously, you have disqualified me as a helper for you. Now you can dismiss me and continue your old ways.

HE: No. It will be different. This time I will be strong. I lacked the will power before but now I have really made a decision and with a little more will power, I think I can make it stick.

I: You talk like God Almighty.

HE: Me? God? I am just a man. A little bit the worse for my drinking, but only a man. But I have this disease—alcoholism. The American Medical Association calls it a disease. It is. There is something wrong with my body chemistry. That is why I drink. Alcoholics Anonymous calls it a disease, too. I look into things. I learn from what I read.

I: I think your point is that you are a well-informed and reasonable man.

HE: I am!

I: But why do you make me your opponent? You struggle with me like a wounded bear.

HE: We are not fighting. I agree with some. I reject the rest.

I: It is true, John, that we will always be good friends, no matter how we disagree. But we do disagree sharply on your problem.

Note that this man took a position over authority and in this sense, over God, in the arrogant manner in which he presents himself. As a pastor, I tried to represent to this man an authority (God) other than his own authority. There is a straight line, I am suggesting, between this man's disdain of pastoral counsel and his rejection of God's authority. This is quickly verified simply by recalling that *no one but John* tells John what to do. Lately, by the grace of God, this man came to a better mind and eventually surrendered to God through me. In surrendering to terms other than his own, he came to know God in a personal way.

Before turning to some final examples of self-enthronement, I call attention, parenthetically, to a most interesting phenomenon which happens to our alcoholic patients[5] who voluntarily submit themselves to the authority of the hospital staff. *They lose their compulsion to drink.* And all this happens within about ten days after admission, even before our active treatment program has begun! These men lose their driving desire. Even if a drink were offered to them, I am sure that most would decline it. One of our former patients told me an interesting tale which verifies this point. This man was thrown into jail for drinking. While in jail, he decided to seek treatment at our hospital, and spoke of his intention to his fellow inmate.

The inmate was aroused by the information. "Yeah—I was there once. Say—I want to tell you where I hid a bottle of wine there. I didn't use it, understand. I just wanted it around. You'll find it buried in the grass of the miniature golf course."

My friend related that when he arrived at the hospital, he lost no time in locating that bottle. But he, too, did not drink the wine. "I did not *need* to have it. There was no compulsion to drink. It was just comforting to know it was there. I replaced the bottle in its hiding place." This was, perhaps, a dozen years ago and the story is factual to this point.

It has become a legend at the Institute that even today, somewhere on that golf course there is a well-concealed bottle of sherry wine around which alcoholic patients gather on moonlit nights. Each man is said to lovingly hold that bottle, look at it admiringly and then pass it to the next man. But no man has ever been seen taking a drink from that bottle, according to the legend. An exhaustive search was made for the bottle and though none was ever found, the legend persists. And I hope it long continues because it neatly illustrates my point—that a voluntary subjection to an authority structure (the hospital) neutralizes the compulsion to drink.

There is better evidence than a legend, however, on which to base this assertion. I have observed this very same phenomenon clinically in a prostitute, who, when she stayed at our hospital for a time, lost her desire to be promiscuous; in neurotic people suffering from compulsions who, when they became hospitalized, were no longer so compulsive; in drug addicts who, under hospitalization, could not imagine why they wanted to shoot heroin.

How do we account for this? It would seem that health is a state granted to those who voluntarily live under authority whereas

---

[5] The author is Protestant Chaplain at the N. J. Neuro-Psychiatric Institute at Princeton, N. J.

illness is a consequence of ultimatizing one's self in the world. This is consistent with the insight of the Scriptures which consistently connect sin (the essence of which is egocentricity and arrogant pride) with illness.

We find another striking example of egoism in the Holy Scriptures. Turn to the life of the Apostle Peter. Prior to Pentecost, Peter was an enthroned egoist. The gospel of Matthew reveals this fact. "From that time Jesus began to show his disciples that he must go to Jerusalem and suffer many things from the elders and chief priests and scribes, and be killed, and on the third day be raised. And Peter took him and began to rebuke him, saying 'God forbid, Lord! This shall never happen to you' " (Matthew 16:21, 22).

Had we been able to ask Peter, at the time he spoke these words, whether he felt like an arrogant person, he would surely have denied it. Quite to the contrary, Peter would have registered feelings of being small, helpless, and fearful. He would have told us that he felt insecure and anxious about his Lord. Interestingly, the Lord did not share Peter's viewpoint, for Peter is severely rebuked with the words: "Get behind me, Satan! You are a hindrance to me; for you are not on the side of God, but of men" (Matthew 16:23). These words can teach us to beware of the "humility" of the egoist. There is nothing more prideful than the "humility" of a proud man.

I recall a man who began his tale of woe saying: "I am nothing but a no-good bum. I am a human reject, a worthless castoff." This was said to attest his penitence and evoke my sympathy. It did neither for I hear these words as throne-talk. This is a boundlessly self-pitying man who yet presumes to make a judgment about himself which not even Almighty God would make! Who gave this man the right to say this about himself? *He* did—he, the highest power in his world.

Many more examples of ego enthronement could be given. Consider the things we ordinary people say to each other every day.

"What I need is will power. I can whip this problem if I just set my mind to it." This was said by an alcoholic who even today is a practicing alcoholic.

"The whole trouble with me is my wife. Why did I ever marry that witch? Someday I'll change her or die trying." This marital war continues without abatement.

"I'm *not* going to drink that milk and I don't care if Daddy spanks me all night for it!" This was said by a child. We expect this of a child but as the child grows older, we also expect him to learn obedience to lawful authority.

"The doctor said this illness was very serious but they can't kill an old horse. I've got a lot of mileage left in me!" I officiated at the funeral of this "brave" man a week after he made the statement.

When the ego is on the throne, God is dethroned. When the ego is under the authority and power of God, God is King. Our *ideas* about God, though important, should not be given a primary position in our lives. Modern Christianity has theologized so much about the nature of God that today most Christians have only an idea-God. The God of the New Testament is a power-authority-God. What that means concretely is that the early Christians cut out a large place at the very center of their lives for God and enthroned Him as *Lord*. It was later that the church became a haven for bright minds who gave impressive displays of erudite theology on the nature of God. Some of this was perhaps needed, but it was a great tragedy that God became Someone to understand rather than the Power-to-heal-and-save in surrendered lives.

Today we desperately need to know God in terms of His Lordship over us. I am constantly amazed how alcoholics in Alcoholics Anonymous submit to God as *Lord,* no matter what their denominational creed. I have seen Roman Catholics, Jews, Protestants and even a few atheists, all find the one true God as they "admitted I was powerless under alcohol and came to believe in a power higher than myself" (Step One). I am convinced that this approach of AA *works*. It brings a transformation as a result of the repositioning of a person under God. It also brings sobriety.

I was at one time very critical of AA for its description of God as Higher Power or God "as we understand Him." No longer. Everyone has a faulty concept of God, even our best theologians. Who are we to point the finger at one who is beginning to find God, telling him that his ideas about this new Power are faulty? These ideas will change as the relationship develops. There will come a day, hopefully, when God is known as revealed in Jesus Christ, but meanwhile, AA points us in the right direction—surrender to Higher Power with the consequent dethronement of the human ego.

Sophisticated, formal theology which I or the person I am helping possess, may be intellectually stimulating but it is nonessential. We do not need it. I have never yet seen a suffering person really helped by understanding that God is the Ground of our Being, or even, for that matter, that God is dead. Although I cite these two examples of theology from the liberal wing of the church, the "right" ideas about God of many evangelicals are quite as useless. When we try to put God down on paper, all we do is build a monument to our intellectual cleverness.

I know that we in the Reformed branch of Christianity have always prided ourselves in "serving God with our minds." But really, is it not time to stop these pleasant but nonproductive exercises? While the world literally goes to hell, we sit in our book-lined studies pondering the chief end of man—"to know God and enjoy him forever." God is not a tricky puzzle to figure out; nor is He a neat piece of art to admire. He is a Worker-King.

God is working for the overthrow of the pretender to the throne of the human heart. God sees how we image-bearers have chosen to enthrone our own egos. He sees our pretense of pseudo-divinity, our vanity, our delusion of omnipotence.

But is this really an accurate picture of the state of our hearts? Listen to the testimony of a man who has looked deeply into the human heart. Dr. Eric Berne, a Freudian psychiatrist, speaks of three basic beliefs in all people. Everyone believes in "the immortality of his being, the irresistibility of his charms, and the omnipotence of his thoughts and feelings."[6] When Dr. Berne refers to our universal belief in the immortality of our being, he means that we are so self-oriented that our minds will not tolerate the thought that once we were not, and that someday we will not be. Countless people have and will slip away into death still holding a deep conviction that "this can't be happening to me. To others, yes. But not me. Something will still happen to save me." Dr. Berne also sees, particularly in our dreams, how each person has such a deep conviction of his exquisite charm that he believes he is downright irresistible to others! Also worth pondering is our secret belief that our thoughts and feelings can wield an all-powerful, magical influence over our world.

The good Lord is long-suffering and kind. He *must* be to put up with our kind of thinking. One prophet after another has been sent to open our eyes. Isaiah, for example, saw the problem crystal clear when he said: "All we like sheep have gone astray; we have turned every one to his own way . . ." (Isaiah 53:6). Jeremiah came to a similar conclusion: "The heart is deceitful above all things, and desperately corrupt; who can understand it?" (17:9).

If Jeremiah could not understand the human heart, I am sure we will not. We can, however, like Jeremiah, describe its strange patterns of behavior. To do that we will need to see and think

---

[6] Eric Berne, *A Layman's Guide to Psychiatry and Psychoanalysis,* New York: Simon and Schuster, 1957, p. 27.

about specific, real-life, modern examples of "going our own way," as Isaiah puts it. I realize I run a risk in the next few chapters of offending you, perhaps even depressing you. I promise, however, to eventually lead you out of all this "bad news" to the Good News of Christ.

4. The ultimatized man

"In every heart there is a cross and a throne and each is occupied. If Jesus is on the throne, ruling, self is on the cross, dying. But if self is being obeyed, and so is ruling, then it is on the throne. And self on the throne means that Jesus has been put on the cross.[1]

"We deceive ourselves about our selfishness and egocentricity because we are afraid a revelation of our true nature would alienate us from our chosen associates. Further, we cannot face the Biblical implication that the true nature of man is such that each of us is really engaged (however unconsciously) in the building of the kingdom of Keith or Joe (or whatever *your* name is). . . . To build up our images, and our kingdoms, we are subtly dishonest about any thoughts or desires or habits we have which do not fit our projected image for fear our subjects will discover our secret; that inside, behind the facade, we are not really kingly or queenly at all; but instead in our intimate actions we are the servants, the slaves, of our resentments, our jealousies, our lusts, and our anxieties, and insecurities. And the more kingly, the more self-sufficient an image we try to project, the more we must dishonestly deny in a hundred ways that we are self-centered little children at heart bent on our own self-gratification."[2]

Each of us "creates" his own world. That is, we set certain things up in life the way we want them. Characteristically, we give a place in our world to ourselves first, then to other people, and only then to God who, quite honestly, will have to be satisfied with

---

[1] S. D. Gordon, *Quiet Talks on Prayer,* New York: Grosset and Dunlap, 1903, p. 109.
[2] Keith Miller, *The Taste of New Wine* (Waco, Texas: Word Books, 1965), pp. 26, 27. Used by permission of the publisher.

what little corner we can find for Him. Since God makes no audible complaint and because other people are creating the very same kind of world along with us, we feel reasonably comfortable about continuing this mad operation which is doomed to end in disaster.

As each of us insistently continues our course of folly, it becomes apparent that the world as shaped by each person, is an insulting caricature of the way God intended the world to be. Squarely on the top of man's world is a throne on which man sits, self-coronated. In such a world, man the egoist

(1) ultimatizes himself,
(2) lives in conflict with people and
(3) ignores God.

Let us in this chapter look at our tendency to ultimatize ourselves. I will attempt to describe what is commonly found in varying degrees in all people, whether one is on the back ward of a mental hospital or just-doing-well-thank-you in society. I speak about you. I speak about myself.

"My feelings determine what I do"

We quickly develop in our lives a fascination with our personal powers. Among these powers is the power of feeling. Some of our most basic feelings are anger and fear. The force of these feelings within us is astonishing both to us and to others. When these feelings hit us, it seems we are being pushed by a massive power much greater than us. They seem quite beyond our power to control. It *seems* that way; yet the power source for these feelings is the person himself.

One can develop his life in such a way that his feelings are ultimate. This is what is meant by the "modern enthronement of feeling" (A. A. Schneiders). Our feelings can be worshiped, as they often are, for example, in the modern theater where the mark of an acceptable actor is that he has feeling, does his work with feeling and creates a feeling in his audience. The world of feelings is also given an ultimate position in the work of most psychologists and psychiatrists. They work hard to get a person to express his feelings, to feel he can cope with a situation and above all, to feel better about himself. Indeed, most of us, as we saw in Chapter 1, live under the impression that our feelings are *us*. It follows that *we* are not going to do anything until *we* feel like it. To act without a wholehearted feeling of wanting to do the act is thought to be hypocritical. "Why, I would feel like a hypocrite if I turned the cheek when someone attacks me. If I did, I would do it only because of someone else. Frankly, I don't feel that way. You would not want me to be a hypocrite, would you?" And so, never having the feeling, this person never acts. He chooses to live under the tyranny of his feelings, a tyranny his own egoism establishes.

The "ultimate" mind

What one egoist does with his feelings, another may do with the power of his intellect. We all know people who are absolutely fascinated with their brains. It is their most prized possession, simply because it computes a little faster and a little better than ordinary brains. People with lower IQ's than the self-styled intelligentsia seem dull, even dead, because "the brain" needs someone to compete with him in his contest of information swapping. So many of our conversations degenerate into competitive word games which have nothing at all to do with friendship and the enjoyment of persons. There *is* such a thing as pride of intellect and the tragedy of it is that this is another way in which a person creates his own world with his own ego placed squarely in the center of it.

The "ultimate" strength

So also with will power. I have watched, for example, well-meaning people advise their dying dear ones to fight to live. The unspoken assumption of this advice was that the dying person held his destiny in his own hands and all he had to do to stay around was to use his will power. Will power is also supposed to keep alcoholics from drinking, husbands faithful to their wives and neurotics free from depression. But will power does not solve any of these problems. That is because will power is always *I* centered. If we were more accurate, we would speak of *I* will power. Now if an "I" is a source of power unto himself, there is no need to appeal to Higher Power. The one excludes the other. More will need to be said in Chapter 6 about the fallibility of will power, but for the present, it is sufficient to note that the ultimatized man treasures it as one of his dearest possessions.

Several friends have been very frank in telling me that I am much too hard here on will power. The preceding paragraph, they tell me, is far too absolutistic because it leaves no real place for any will power in our lives and that seems very much like advising a person to be completely inert and passive.

My friends are right. Obviously, there are things within the range of humanly possible things which we should do. It *is* possible for a sick person to call a doctor, for an alcoholic to seek out AA, for a husband and wife in marital conflict to seek counsel and, for a neurotic person to take his medication. The Serenity Prayer urges us to "change the things I can." The problem arises when we use will power on "the things I cannot change." Here I take an absolutistic position, arguing that we should not use even a "little bit" of will power in the solution of these impossible problems. It is impossible for a sick person to simply will his recovery; it is impossible for an alcoholic to control his alcohol problem with will power; it is impossible for us to lay down, unaided, our really deep resentments; it is impossible for a neurotic person to fight against and prevail over his illness. And yet, these are precisely the tasks which the egoist in us assigns to us. The humanly impossible problems can be solved, but God alone can do it.

"Everything happens to me"

Another mark of the egocentric person is his tendency to personalize any number of things which happen to him in the course of his life. Whatever happens is always viewed as being for or against him as a person. If a storm blows a few shingles off his house, it happened because a cruel fate had determined that he was born under the wrong sign of the Zodiac. It does not occur to him that the shingles were simply weak and worn-out. It was an act of fate against *him*. Or again, if the rain stops just as our friend is about to begin a picnic supper, he announces to his family that the only way he can account for such a happy coincidence is that "he lives right" and "somebody up there likes him." The events in the world are always classified either against him or for him. He who sits enthroned is the crucial person in such a world.

The feeling of being in control

As the egoist sits on his throne high in the heavens of his mind, he senses an exhilarating power to rule his world. It is as though he lives in a push-button universe. When the egoist pushes a button, something is supposed to happen. If nothing happens, he reaches for the panic button (God), hopefully, to make the world behave itself the way it should.

The word *control* is very dear to anxious, neurotic people. The failure to control life explains why people break down. When a person has a nervous breakdown, the feeling of it is something like this:

> I am coming apart at the seams, losing control of myself. I can't bring myself to think as I should and even at such times as I think straight, I can't bring myself to act as I would like to. It's as though my mind says one thing, my feelings another and my will, still another. I am out of control. That's serious

enough. But worse, my world is out of control. People are not co-operating with me. Even events seem to conspire against me. Time is another problem. I seem to always be working against it. I wish I could be strong and control my nerves and my situation, but the more I try, the worse it becomes.

This suffering soul lives in a self-created world in which he alone feels responsible for *making* things happen. He leaves no room for *letting* things happen, for that would mean that he would be *under* control and that a power outside himself would be trusted to act upon his world. If healing and health are to come, our neurotic person will need to resign as manager of the universe and hand the controls over to God. Instead of praying for God to save him or give him strength to fight his problems, this man would then pray that the Father's will would be done in his life; that whatever comes, it be accepted as God's will. A prayer such as this would indicate that the man had surrendered the controls of his life to the Highest Power.

A corollary to the egoist's insistence on controlling his world, is that *his* terms must prevail. Of course, that is impossible to consistently achieve, so when he fails to live life on his terms, he will collect tons of resentment. The point to observe here is that the egoist has no place in his life for a *voluntary* submission to the terms of others. He *may* submit but it would then be done either with resentment, or because it is in the nature of a deal ("I'll submit but only to achieve something that means so much to me that I will bear the indignity of doing what you suggest"), or both.

Listen to the insistent terms of a "broken" alcoholic.

HE: I have come to this hospital to get reasons why I drink. I want to be told what is wrong with me. But I'll be darned if I am going to share my story with these other alcoholics.

I: You come, then, with your terms spelled out. You want to ignore the others.

HE: Their problems are no concern of mine. I am not going to confess my feelings to the world. I hope we are not disagreeing too greatly.

I: There is a sharp difference between us.

HE: A difference of theory.

I: You use nice words. We flatly disagree on the approach to your problem.

HE: There are many approaches to any problem.

I: But there is only one way *out* of your problem. Do you want it or not?

HE: Of course I want it. I need help to stop my drinking.

I: On your terms or mine?

HE: On *open* terms.

I: You are dancing around me.

HE: You have not given me an outline of your approach.

I: You want a road map before you begin. And you want proof.

HE: I want directions.

I: You want your terms. You do not freely submit to anything. You have your ideas. They are set. You want me to come to your terms.

HE: No, you are the teacher. I am the pupil.

I: Are you serious?

HE: Yes.

I: If I asked you to stand in the corner of this room, facing the wall for a period of ten minutes because I assured you it would do some good, would you do it? Would you follow me even if it seems foolish to you?

HE: If I were of the opinion it would benefit me, yes. I expect a little map. I'll accept anything. What I want is to be shown a direct road. You have not shown it to me.

The purpose of this kind of dialogue is to set the stage for a person to surrender. The surrender is to God through a human person. Had this person surrendered through me, I would have immediately brought him to God by suggesting, first, that an honest, moral inventory be made to God in the presence of a third party, and second, that he offer prayer with that third party for a knowledge of God's will for his life. I see my task as a pastor to assist but yet keep getting out of the way of the drama which is taking place between God and the surrendered person.

But surrender—and that in concrete ways—it must be, if a man is to be saved from defeat. I think of surrender, somewhat crudely, by imagining a copilot in an airliner who has lost his way while in command of the plane. The captain, however, knows where he is and how to pilot the plane to safety. The copilot, if he is to be saved, must surrender the controls to the pilot. Imagine what would happen if the copilot insisted on keeping one hand on the controls while the captain set the plane back on course. Disaster would follow. One person must be in control. Either the pilot's terms must prevail or the copilot's. But the copilot is not doing so well. He will have to make up his mind either to trust the captain or, trusting himself, crash.

The feeling of being righteous

Let us now look at a fourth characteristic of the self-enthroned person. He has a deep conviction of his righteousness (and the unrighteousness of others). He *must* believe this, for to doubt it is to risk becoming just another man among men. Besides, it does no good to the ego of a king to admit that he is guilty of wrong doing. Consequently, he sets up his world so that he is the "white guy" and other people are varying shades of gray and black.

As a counseling pastor, I see this numerous times in couples who are in marital strife. Almost invariably, each party feels righteous and the only problem seems to be that the *other* party is not shaping up. If one party in the marriage would only say: "Honey, you are right. I was wrong and I'll change my behavior," they would never come for counsel because the game of hate-trading usually ends the moment one party refuses to play. But each feels no need to change. In such a situation, I often turn to the one who I suspect is least egocentric and ask this person if he cares to speak about any of his own shortcomings and faults. The answers I receive most frequently are:

"The trouble with me is that I am too honest."

"The trouble with me is that I am too sensitive, too easily hurt."

"Well, I can't think of anything important offhand—oh, a lot of little things, but getting back to my wife...."

Such "confessions" only skim the surface of the problem. Indeed, there is dishonesty here but let me quickly add that this dishonesty is unconscious to the person. True, the gross naïveté is many times unbelievable to those who discern the delusion, but again, most times a person is simply following whatever light he can see.

This is a good place to say that this naïve unawareness is something which characterizes almost all the thinking and actions of the egocentric man. Not one of us consciously sets out on a certain day to play god. It is a pattern of life which we not only fall into quite unawares in childhood but which remains largely hidden to our consciousness in the adult years. Until, that is, someone makes our egocentricity known to us. I invariably find that when this is done—and it should *never* be done until a person asks for an opinion—that a person will either flatly disbelieve it, or, buying it, be surprised to a point of embarrassment. If the one offering the enlightenment will communicate that he understands that the person did not know what he was doing, thus avoiding all accusation and judgment, a spirit of helpfulness and understanding will ensue.

The feeling of being right

There is another feeling which invariably accompanies the feeling of being righteous and that is the conviction of being right. We saw this clearly in Chapter 3 in the case of Bob—the man who found it so unbearable to be wrong, that he called into question even the reliability of the dictionary. There is no need to further elaborate on this except to point out that this rigid conviction of being right is shared not only by the more arrogant and outspoken type of person but as much by the compliant, soft-spoken person who freely admits to being an "unworthy sinner." He likes to give the impression that he was wrong and now, in all "humility," freely confesses his sin and error. This is the *mea culpa* ("I am a sinner") phenomenon which we see so often in religious people.

The only problem is that there is nothing religious about it because it is saturated with arrogance. The "virtue" of *mea culpa* is that by maneuvering into a position where one can become self-accusatory (himself choosing a particular accusation and the moment to disclose it) he not only stays in control and continues on his own terms but also protects himself from any accusation from without. It is a fantastically smooth way to be a winner.

One hesitates to disturb the self-satisfied feelings of a person who is so comfortably defended by his *mea culpa* attitude, but such is necessary if any real growth is to take place. A pastor might do this by suggesting to his parishioner, now that he realizes that he has done something wrong, that he take steps to redress his wrong through apology and restitution. As soon as the "penitent" hears these suggestions from without—that is, suggestions originating from another person—he usually begins to hedge, even retract and maneuver into a position where he can follow his *own* suggestions. The insistent claim of the egoist is that he originate any ideas which will be put into action in his life. It is sensed as an indignity to the "king" to be dependent upon the thinking of others. Unoriginal ideas are not only untrustworthy but they also mar, even if ever so slightly, the glorious beauty of the king's thoughts!

Homemade laws

The position of the egoist which began with a conviction of righteousness is accompanied, as we saw, with a conviction of being right. Something else follows with inexorable logic—something which astonishes and frightens us. The next step is that *the self-enthroned person becomes a law unto himself.* He makes himself a moral code! Why not? He feels righteous. He feels he is right.

This does not mean that every egoist now becomes a hardened

criminal. Many do, but most of us are much too crafty to spend our lives in jail. No, the majority of us will submit to the law of the land (and perhaps even to the laws of God) because it is prudential to do so. But that will not deter us from going to the limits of the law and living over the law whenever possible. We will do whatever we can get away with. Within that limitation, we set out to do whatever we wish to do, so long as no one gets hurt, or, if someone does, we make sure he does not make too much fuss about it. This attitude is not wrong because it is prudential but because it is crafted by that clever egoism in us which will submit to no law or standard other than those of our own making. In Chapter 7, we will again look at the problem of law in the world of the egoist, but here I wish to point out a final characteristic in us as we try to ultimatize ourselves in the world.

A life of worry and frenzy

The enthroned egoist is often a very grim person who assaults life with energetic, yet purposeless activity and busyness. Inwardly, he is desperate. And serious. He feels that his life demands his constant attention. To relax, to let things happen, to stop worrying and take a nap—these suggestions are abhorrent to his life. He is eternally busy, working and worrying his way through life. He feels it all depends on *him*.

With such feelings, we can understand why we adopt activisim as a style of life. We throw all our energy into the struggle. We never finish our work. It lies there, beckoning us, we always feel, to greater efforts. God knows we *work*. He sees how we try to push all the buttons but little happens. Our anxiety grows. If it cripples us we stimulate ourselves with pep pills. If we are hyperactive, we sedate ourselves with alcohol and tranquilizers. *Anything* to put us back into the position of being in control.

The problem, however, is that we were never intended to be *in* control. There is seldom anything functionally wrong with us as people. It is simply that we get ourselves into the wrong position. We are like a passenger on an airplane who, having bound and gagged the pilot, attempts to fly the plane himself. He soon finds, to his sorrow, that he does not know enough about flying to keep the plane under control. Our new pilot is becoming anxious, understandably. He begins to turn the knobs of the control panel. Perspiration is cascading down his cheeks. He is presently the world's busiest, most serious and most foolish man! His only hope lies in asking the captain to take over the controls. If our mutinous passenger is to be saved, he must get back into his assigned seat, buckle his seat belt as the other passengers have done, and behave himself.

5. Living against people

We are still looking at some of the chief characteristics of you and me as we construct our egocentric worlds. A very large part of that world is people. Fact is, our problems in life would be very few and those very minor if it were not for people. But God so planned human life that we live in community. At present we are observing how it is that we come into conflict with our fellows. My purpose is to show that much of what people do in their relationships with others is a direct result of the egocentric shape into which they have formed their world. Consider now four characteristic operations which the egoist uses in human relationships: (1) he seeks to "win" over others in contests; (2) he may seek to elevate himself but without engaging in contests; (3) he may seek to destroy his fellows, and (4) he may choose to withdraw from the world of people.

THE WINNING LOSER

The egoist, because he lives above people, must constantly live in opposition to his fellows since they form a constant threat to his position. Quite simply, he does not trust people. This is the very same problem as the "king of the mountain" game many of us played as children. When a truck dumped a load of sand or stone, one of us would run to the top and shout, "I'm the king of the mountain!" Immediately the playmates of the king would contest his position. It was the task of the king to kick away all pretenders to the throne. The vigilance and strength of the king seldom proved sufficient to a many-sided attack and so, invariably, the king would fall in ignominious defeat as the victors shouted, "The king is dead!"

This type of interpersonal contest explains, it seems to me, why we often view people in general through a negative screen. People seem a problem. We find them too much to handle. Even our greetings to them may have a ring of insincerity because the presence of people demands that we deal with them and handle them, usually in a competitive or at least in a defensive fashion.

I see this problem constantly among professional people. Antagonistic living seems to have particular appeal to the highly educated. We frequently spend our final days of learning in graduate school. After that, we only teach, never learn. But what I wanted to say was that professional people are highly competitive. A pastor, for example, is seldom ready to learn from another pastor. Characteristically, we relate to each other by withdrawing from or competing with each other. The gathering of pastors into a synod, for example, is frequently the setting and signal for intense rivalry and power-grabbing to begin among certain delegates who, the day before, appointed themselves to high office. Not all the delegates do this, however. The remainder of us sit by the hour in silent disgust and nurse along the resentments we have toward the leaders. It takes many of us two or three days of rest to recover from this sort of ordeal!

It is the same with my friends who are psychologists. Most psychologists feel quite warmly toward pastors. Religion does not form a particular threat to psychology and that makes for a noncompetitive, reasonably warm relationship. I know a very distinguished psychologist who, when he speaks to pastors is delightful, warmly human and genuinely helpful. The moment this man is with his psychologist colleagues, he becomes arrogant, pedantic, distrustful and very overbearing. How do we explain this flip? Why would a psychologist (or a pastor) become competitive with his peers but toward "outsiders" and "undersiders" show genuine love? I suggest that it has much to do with our egoistical aspirations. They constantly bring us into a needless, foolish competition with other persons.

The egoist, therefore, insists on winning. So long as he can convince himself that he is a victor, he feels good. Even in such a small matter as playing a game, he is out to win. Winning is a testimony to him that his egoistic style of life is working. Even a game, perhaps with children, must bear such news to him and for that reason, he plays to win even against his own children who are at a decided disadvantage. Any loss is hard to take. Losing a game, a competitive sale, an argument, a member of one's family— these things are accepted, but never without resentment and the plan, if possible, to retaliate.

In all this "winning," the self-enthroned person is really the loser. He is a winning loser and this suggests that a better way would be to become a losing winner. It is precisely what our Lord taught us: "He who finds his life will lose it, and he who loses his life for my sake will find it" (Matthew 10:39).

One-upmanship

A maneuver similar to this competitive struggle is the phenomenon of one-upmanship. This particular type of egoistic urge comes to expression in varied ways. We see it sometimes in the way a seminarian who is learning the art of counseling will try to anticipate and guess the feelings of a parishioner before these feelings have come to conscious awareness. At times, a student-pastor with a few psychology courses under his belt, will privately predict the behavior of a parishioner. If any part of the prediction comes true, it registers with the seminarian as a well-deserved confirmation of his ability to be "one up" on the parishioner. It is a delicious feeling.

One-upmanship is common in marriage. One woman told me that she made it a practice to always outthink and outguess her husband. She tried to "keep one step ahead of him." That way she could be prepared to handle him. Obviously, she was out to run the marriage according to her plans and specifications. Her only problem was a husband who had lost interest in her. One can see why!

We find an example of one-upmanship in much today that passes for scholarship. Many modern scholars put forth vast amounts of effort to smash popular caricatures, destroy old "myths," and set forth enlightened perspectives. One scholar out-does another in this delightful game of one-upmanship. New statistics are brought forth. Research grants are obtained and old theories debunked. In their place we would hope for new answers, but what we get are new questions intended to be a bit more clever than questions others have raised. It is scholarly to raise new, interesting questions and steer clear of any answers.

One soon learns on the wards of a mental hospital that not a few of our patients have had their breakdowns because they were the losers in the game of one-upmanship. Perhaps a majority of them want to build up their strength and try once again to win when they leave. A precious minority—a remnant—are ready to get out of this sick game. They are desperately tired of brain games and "brilliant" solutions. These chosen few are ready to live *with* people *under* God —that Person who alone has the right to be one up on us.

One-downmanship

Those who abhor the aggressive haughtiness of one who tries to be "one up" on his fellows, may prefer a form of one-downmanship in their dealings with others. Sometimes we see this in the lives of people with overt criminal tendencies. They will often seek to outdo each other by "going one further" than others in the direction of lawlessness. Still another person with such tendencies will say: "Well, my reputation was ruined, so I figured I might as well *really* show the world how to raise hell."

Closely akin to this, and hardly more virtuous, is the "religious" person who delights in speaking about his sins, his accursedness and depravity. Such a person may not only say that he is a sinner but that he is the greatest of sinners and, if he is really enthroned, claim to be an unpardonable sinner. Religious people find this a favorite device for establishing a certain uniqueness about themselves. It is a secretly enjoyable kind of self-effacement. We seem to get a good feeling from feeling bad about our sins. Have not we all felt properly penitential and even *better* by repeating Sunday after Sunday the Prayer of Confession:

"We have erred and strayed from thy ways. . . .
We have left undone those things we ought to have done;
And we have done those things which we ought not to have done;
There is no health in us . . . miserable offenders."

General confessions usually are too general to do us any real good, save that they make us feel a little more aware of our sins than other people and that sounds very much like a form of pharisaic one-downmanship. I know that if I have a parishioner seeking my counsel who says: "I have sinned. I am a sick, evil man. I am a miserable offender," I will not encourage him to a greater appreciation of himself as the world's worst. What I might do is suggest that he please specify his sins, confess them to God and make amends to those he has wronged. This usually evokes a recital of his so-called virtues, thereby at least disposing of his sense of one-downmanship. But not really, because one-upmanship and one-downmanship are the same thing—a mispositioned person in the world.

WINNING WITHOUT CONTESTS

The judgmental spirit

So far we have spoken of the urge to "win" in contests with people. Some of us do not care for competition because it entails many risks for our egos and we would rather not compete than possibly lose. This attitude does not prohibit us, however, from elevating ourselves above our fellows. One of our favorite ways of doing this is to become judgmental of others. Remembering that the egoist loves to think of himself as being over people and morally white, we can sympathize with his understandable urge to become a judge over people.

Our judge, sad to say, soon runs into problems. The people under him, for one thing, have their own ideas about who should be appointed judge and they threaten rebellion. What bothers them particularly about the present, self-appointed regime is the grossly impossible expectations of the judge. Under the standards he sets up for others, no one could measure up. He expects perfect performance on the part of his fellow man but is most indulgent and understanding of his own shortcomings.

As the judge becomes older, the tendency to judge and condemn may become more accentuated. A favorite target is the younger generation which, if we are to take the egoist's point of view, is just not measuring up. Young people today are in a state of decadence—why, just look at their hair, their clothes, their morals and listen to their songs. We should add, incidentally, that an additional characteristic of the aging egoist is that he easily forgets his own youth.

The judgmental spirit we are describing should not be confused with appropriate forms of judgment. It is appropriate that a judge in a court of law come to a decision on a case. Juries should hand down verdicts. Doctors should diagnose illness. Pastors have not only a right to an opinion in certain ecclesiastical matters but also jurisdiction. Legitimate judges are appointed to office with the consent of the governed. Such judges still run the danger of misusing their office but at its best, every precaution is taken to eliminate their self-interest, thereby benefiting those who are under their jurisdiction. The judgmental person, on the other hand, satisfies his own perverted needs, leaving the judged without any real benefit.

The professorial spirit

As we saw previously, it is but a short step for one to move from a conviction of being righteous to a position of being right. When the egoist takes this step, as he characteristically does, he adds the role of teacher to that of a judge. Thereafter, the egoist seldom really learns. He now speaks in a professorial manner to people. It seems to be an especial affliction among us clergymen.

Frequently, when pastors gather in groups, we come together to get our points across to our less enlightened brethren. Now only a fool would explicitly take such a position and we are not fools. We prefer to present ourselves as humble learners to our colleagues. In speaking, we take pains to point out how little we know about spiritual matters, how tentatively our conclusions should be treated, how precious is the wisdom of the Fathers and Brethren, *et cetera*. This looks very humble—until a colleague attempts to decrease the ignorance of the pastor by presenting some facts and information which will enlarge his knowledge. Suddenly our humble pastor speaks with the authority of the *Encyclopaedia Britannica*—he has been misunderstood. This often develops into a feeling of being attacked, and so the battle continues *ad nauseam*. The "teacher" is obviously trying to make the point that though it is true that he knows nothing, nobody else does either! In this way he retains his teacher status, even though it is in the field of ignorance.

The silent loner

Our last example of self-elevation is drawn from experience with groups. Consider the silent member. He does not speak unless spoken to. He is a spectator, listening, even enjoying the group experience, but he remains aloof and withdrawn. What is he doing? There are many who feel this person was the victim of faulty group experiences in his youth. He has never learned how to relate to people. This is a very sentimental but unfortunately not a helpful point of view.

The isolated group member is more helpfully seen, I have found, by understanding that aloofness is his way of giving himself special character status. Other group members involve themselves and interact. The silent, aloof member is a parasite. He invests little, risks little, but draws much from the group. Added to this is the ego-satisfying feeling of winning. In a counseling group, all are expected to participate. It is an unwritten contract between the members. The detached person wishes to make an exception of himself, thereby scoring another victory.

When this maneuver is brought to the attention of the silent loner in a helpful, loving way which is free from all judgment, he most frequently reacts with a feeling of complete surprise and, perhaps, some anger because he has been discerned. If God has brought this man to a point of readiness to change, he will buy the invitation of the group to involve himself and interact. In doing this, the group member does a profoundly spiritual act. He begins to live *with* people *under* a Higher Power in a context of accomplished forgiveness.

The Urge to Destroy Others

Let us see now how the egoist intends destruction upon the heads of those who cross him. Perhaps the favorite response of an enthroned person is to retaliate by aiming some hate at the objectionable person. The depths of hatred in each of us is frightening. The manufacture of hate is our oldest accomplishment. We have practiced it since our first diaper became wet.

Resentment

Most frequently we see hate in the form of resentment. Of all the destructive things (other than guilt, but this may also be a form of anger) we can do to ourselves, I know of none so damaging as resentment. We carefully accumulate it. Strecker and Appel[1] underscore the point that feelings of anger are stored and accumulated, layer upon layer, so to speak. We like to think that anger and hate have evaporated when we are not consciously aware of them, but not so—they are repressed. There are few problems which *all* people have but this is one of them: we all are energetic collectors of resentment, endlessly storing it within us for the time when it will erupt with the regularity of Old Faithful and the violence of Vesuvius.

Resentment is surely one of our biggest problems. Our minds are so bent on self-magnification and self-glory that we become hypersensitive to any sort of slight and overreact even to the smallest provocation. Last evening, for example, I was conversing on the phone with an alcoholic. He asked what I thought he should do in his situation. I advised him to enter a hospital. Was my advice well received? No, it was rejected on the grounds that my counsel was too directive! A little later in the conversation, I happened to clear my throat. I tell you the truth—I was accused of making a disparaging remark!

Perhaps you feel my friend's hypersensitive feeling of resentment was caused by his alcohol. How is it then that we find these very same attitudes in neurotics, drug addicts, people in marital conflict, homosexuals, criminals—indeed, *all* people? It is because all people are struggling with the same basic issue—egoism. Or, it may be that you prefer the Biblical term *sin*. I use the two terms rather interchangeably because the essential feature of both is rebellion against the rule of God.

I suspect that resentment is very much like an iceberg. The largest part is submerged and unseen, but some of it comes to

[1] Edward A. Strecker and K. E. Appel, *Discovering Ourselves,* New York: The Macmillan Co., 1962, pp. 122-129.

visible expression. The similarity ends there, however, because icebergs are not known to attack ships. Resentful people can and do violently assault their fellows either with words (as in character assassination) or in actual deed. It is another result of our egoistic posture in the world. Violence can occur when a resentment is acted out. Here again we see how we have positioned ourselves over and against people rather than with them. We are out to win a victory and destroy our opponent.

Such violence is fueled by resentment. What may have begun in us as a slight irritation can connect with our accumulated store of resentments and from there become a full scale campaign to destroy our opponent and walk away with another "victory" to our credit.

The most popular advice today on the problem of dealing with our resentments is to discharge them in socially approved ways while they are small and manageable. Resentments are then thought of as tiny piles of gunpowder, each of which will make a harmless "pop" when ignited if the pile is small and isolated but a tremendous explosion if gathered together. As I read the Sermon on the Mount, however, the view of our Lord is quite different. He teaches us not to throw fire on any gunpowder, small pile or large. The way to deal with resentment is not by way of emotional explosions but rather *not to collect it in the first place*. Such a statement rests on the assumption that we have a choice of responding to others either with love or hate. These are not automatic unconscious attitude over which we have no control. We are human spirits, not animals. If someone wrongs us, we have a choice either of becoming angry or having some compassion for a person who is in error. Resentment and anger can only lead to retaliation and the escalation of violence. An attitude of compassion, on the other hand, will lead one to do something constructive for the wrongdoer. "Don't allow yourself to be overpowered by evil. Take the offensive—overpower evil with good!" (Romans 12:21, Phillips). "Let there be no more resentment, no more anger or temper, no more violent self-assertiveness, no more slander and no more malicious remarks" (Ephesians 4:31, Phillips). This is the way of nonviolence.

To be sure, I am speaking idealistically. In real life, none of us can avoid feelings of resentment, often expressing them in violent ways. We *do* collect gunpowder and even throw fire on it. We are not saints. What about that?

First, we need to recognize that blocking our resentment and anger will harm us, as the psychologists rightly point out. They give us good advice to sublimate these destructive, anti-social impulses, channeling them into socially approved, constructive action. The anger we inevitably collect, therefore, should be discharged preferably in beneficial ways, but at least in such ways that people are not harmed.

Secondly, remember that we are talking about developing a life-style which will be *predominately* nonviolent. Elements of anger and violence will remain but in the new style of life these reactions become secondary and episodic whereas the predominate response is one of love, forgiveness, compassion and nonviolence.

Finally, consider the wisdom of God in leaving the remnants of "the old Adam" in us. That "old man" in us is a constant reminder that but for the grace of God, we would yet be under the power of our sins. We are humbled (in the sense of being made equal with our fellows) by the realization that none of us are superior as to virtue. Our anger and resentment will always have a place in us. In an instant, the destructive feelings can be kindled and destroy precious people in our lives. In such moments, we once again misposition ourselves in our worlds. The positioned person always remains enough of an egoist to periodically climb back on the throne of God in the mad hope of establishing himself as both judge and executioner, for the dispensing of judgment and punishment are functions of anger and resentment.

Distrustfulness and lack of faith

The egoist is distrustful of all except himself. He will not allow anyone to hold the reins of his life. The control center must be himself. It is weakness, he feels, to be under another's direction. Listen, briefly, to part of a counseling hour in which the egoist's lack of trust is expressed.

He: I'm not at all comfortable with other patients. I guess I just don't know how to love my fellow man.

I: What is wrong with your fellow patients?

He: Want my honest opinion? They are animals! They can't help it but they are!

I: You an animal?

He: Yes, but I can take care of myself. At least I do my share of the work on the ward. The other patients don't do anything. They want to get away with things. Oh, there are two or three who don't. The only thing I really have in common with them is our alcoholism. I know I should not feel that way but I do. Most of those men are lost souls! I try to talk to them but—. I am not nasty to them but I don't mingle.

I: You draw a pretty sharp line between them and you.

HE: I do.

I: You are not a part of them. There is no fellowship.

HE: No. I do my ward work, but I'll be damned if I will teach Smith how to work. I am not his teacher. It is too late to teach Smith. Know what I mean?

I: I know what you mean but do not agree with you.

HE: The only way to teach Smith is by fear.

I: The way you do with animals, huh?

HE: Yes. Yes.

I: Well, that's also the kind of seaman you once were, come to think of it. You were in charge. You were also a dictator and a loner. The problem is that you have become an island in the sea of humanity.

HE: As a seaman, it is true, I ruled. I kept my distance. Come to think of it, I even slept in the fo'c'sle to get away from the men.

I: This isolated you.

HE: I never trusted them. Still do not.

I: John, I have a suggestion. Not a command, just a suggestion. Consider going to our group meeting tomorrow and share with them your feeling that they are animals and that you distrust them.

HE: I would not!

I: Why not be honest? They are in the same boat. They will understand. There is such a need for you to become reconciled to them.

HE: Bring out my problems, huh?

I: Yes. With them.

HE: Let me think about it. I'm not altogether sure I can trust you yet.

I: Take your time.

There is no healing until there is trust. In the ministry of our Lord, the Pharisees constantly sought a sign from Him promising to believe after they would see the miracle they requested. Jesus either denied their request (Mark 8:12) or veiled his answer in such a way that it was not understood (Luke 11:29). Where there was no faith and trust in Christ, there was no sign or help given. In the same way I, representing Christ to my alcoholic brother, seek to call this man to faith in others and ultimately, in God. Once he begins to trust others and God, his addiction will leave him. I have witnessed this miracle from God enough times in those who are sick, to completely accept the words of our Lord: "Your faith has made you well" (Matthew 9:22).

Criticism and apology

Another characteristic in us which testifies to our egoism and its resulting conflict with people, is the inability to receive criticism and offer apology. I treat them as one because both are experienced in the egoist as destructive to himself. Criticism from others, but also self-criticism, usually registers as an attempt to hurt him. This he does not wish to have happen. His delusion of sinlessness is as dear as life itself. Naturally, this excludes the possibility of ever apologizing for a wrong committed.

Think of it—many of us, though we have been extremely devout, never have, nor ever intend to apologize to anyone because we have convinced ourselves that we have nothing for which to apologize! And if, perchance, one can find *one* peccadillo in our life, the need to apologize may then be ruled out because we do not *feel* like apologizing. Unless one has feeling for the apology, it is thought to be hypocritical to go through with it. And God surely does not want us to be hypocrites, does He? When a conversation goes into such channels, one knows the person is in struggle with the massive powers of darkness which God alone is able to subdue.

FLIGHT FROM LIFE

We have attempted in this section to catch glimpses of what ego enthronement does to our relationships with people. At one time we choose to "win" over people; at another time, we will elevate ourselves in an authoritarian manner; at still another time we will seek to destroy people. Let us now add a fourth maneuver—the saddest of them all—our tendency to withdraw from life.

Withdrawing is a form of dying. Our thinking goes something like this—"Since people will not co-operate with me and come to my terms, I will leave them. Hopefully, they will feel guilty for the way they have treated me. It is the only course left whereby I can hope to make them sorry for their cruelty to me."

Vicarious living

The presence of this type of thinking in the suicidal person is obvious, so let us turn to a different type of illustration. I am thinking of a person who chooses to live vicariously as a way of life. I have a friend, a young man in his twenties who has been in a mental hospital since he was twelve. When I questioned his doctor about the prognosis, the doctor shook his head sadly and mumbled, "I doubt that he will ever leave." My friend, however, is a near-genius in two areas: sports and television programs. Do you know how the Chicago White Sox did in the year 1912? Or 1923? He has all this information at his fingertips. This bright young man can give you the plot and characters of almost any television program he has ever seen. He knows the entire sequence of programs throughout the day. Sporting events of any kind are his specialty. I am constantly amazed at the encyclopedic knowledge he possesses on every imaginable athletic contest.

Why does this gifted young man spend his life in a mental hospital? Because he will do nothing else but watch TV. He lives in the world of TV and sports. When the attendant taps him on the shoulder, requesting that he take his turn at mopping the floor, the attendant risks either being tongue-lashed or assaulted. One would think that my friend would like to engage in a game of baseball or touch football. It never happens. This would require that he leave the easy world of TV (games, stories, entertainment) and *do* something in the real world. This is asking too much, he feels. He is content with the world of TV which asks nothing more of him than that he be a silent spectator.

If there is anything which would appeal to the mind of the enthroned egoist, it is the exciting fantasy of sitting on the top of the world, doing nothing but surveying the human scene. Such a person does not need to bother with people, nor is he ever hurt by them. These fantasies are appropriate in a child's world, but when an adult lives vicariously through them, we witness not only a flight from life but the tragic waste of a life misspent.

The world of animals and things

Vicarious living is not the only maneuver we make in withdrawing from people. Consider also how we often retreat from human relationships in order to more safely relate to animals and things. Stanley Harris once said that the real reason people love dogs so much is because they do not criticize us. The same is true of things we cherish. Homes, cars, furniture, jewely, etc., do not speak back to us. They may not always perform the way we wish but at least they do not sass us when we try to shape them up. For this reason alone, animals and things can become very much more dear to us than people. If one, as a way of life, chooses non-people, that person has not only gone contrary to God's established intention with human life, but he also establishes a self-oriented alternative way of life which has no real place for God, and hence no satisfying place in it for any man.

All this because man, in his rebellion, mispositions himself in the world. We have been surveying the damage which this does to us as people. Our folly also affects Deity Himself. To this matter, we now turn.

6. Playing God

Our rebellion against God is, with few exceptions, disguised. It is seldom a rebellion which shouts defiantly into the heavens. We do not think of ourselves as rising up against the Almighty. By the same token, it is rare that we seriously sense a need to surrender to God because it appears to us to be unnecessary. We say to ourselves: "We like God. There is no war between us, surely not on *our* part. We *are* surrendered." Such thoughts soothe us and allow sin to continue because of a deception we have played on ourselves.

I say that few of us see ourselves as people who have assaulted the throne of the Almighty. In truth, we have done something far worse, albeit with fantastic cleverness. Actually, we have chosen to ignore God. We set Him off on the periphery of our self-created world and do not deal with Him except in superficial communication. Before doing this, however, we commit the crime of the ages against God—*we denude Him of His attributes.* We insult God by vesting ourselves with His attributes. We take His holy garments, so to speak, and put them on ourselves. Then we play god.

Do we really do that?

I believe the Bible confirms the truthfulness of the picture I have drawn, if we have ears to hear it. The Bible is constantly pressing home the folly of haughtiness and arrogance. "Thou dost deliver a humble people, but thy eyes are upon the haughty to bring them down" (II Samuel 22:28). "The earth lies polluted under its inhabitants; for they have transgressed the laws, violated the statutes, broken the everlasting covenant" (Isaiah 24:5). "You have lifted up yourself against the Lord of heaven," Daniel told King Nebuchadnezzar in explanation of the coming judgment (Daniel 5:23). But I choose not to present detailed Biblical support for the position that man is in rebellion against God. My point is that we can see in real life the cunning ways in which we arrogantly assume to ourselves the attributes of deity.

Before examples of this are given, I must again state that "playing god" is seldom a deliberate, self-conscious mode of life. Almost invariably, we are unaware of what we are doing. We all possess an incredible amount of genuine naïveté. It is because we cannot see ourselves; we are such poor observers of what we are doing. The word of truth, therefore, must always come from without us. That word of truth must be spoken to each other without judgment or hostility. Only truth spoken in love has a place in any Christian approach to man's dilemma. What each person does to God is terribly serious, and, when we break His commandments, terribly wrong, but the truth is that our deluded minds keep us unaware of our sins. We become "hooked" by our delusions. True, we alone form our delusions but once they are established, we are no longer free, nor aware.

The sense of omnipotence

The attribute of deity which seems to have most appeal to us is *omnipotence,* the fantasy of being all-powerful.

We deeply believe we are.

We bite off things to do which surely must surprise even the Creator of the heavens and the earth. Consider the size of the work-bite in people who work so incessantly that they barely get four hours of sleep a night. "Hard work never hurt anybody. I can take it," we are assured by the loved one who has turned himself into a machine to make money. We live in a day of self-imposed slavery. If anyone would impose an 18-hour day on an employee, he would be taken to court, but so long as the businessman or double-shift worker imposes it on himself, we ask no questions. Were we, however, our brother's keeper, we would ask: Does anyone have the right to place such an unbearable strain on the human body which God has so lovingly created?

Look also at the way we bite off chunks of time which we are never able to chew. Any person overcome with worry will serve as an example. The chronic worrier, though he agrees that "sufficient unto the day is the evil thereof" and though he prays "Give us *this day* our daily bread," still insists on worrying about his job, his marriage, his children, world affairs, a depression. You name it—the worrier has it on his list. There is no place in his world for a living, loving God who takes care of birds, flowers, and, with special concern, people. There is in us this strong urge to fret our way through life. It is our chosen way of yet doing something more in situations where we have reached the limits of what we can do. We assume that if we worry sufficiently, it will become reality. From the beginning, man has said: "Let there be a solution to my problem ..." and to this very day, man still believes that his fiat will bring it about.

The urge to be omnipotent comes to clearest expression when we rely on our will power to deal with the problems of life. Will power is "I" power. It is, we feel, our dearest possession. It is the last thing we surrender because we are very sure that without it we will die. Yet, alcoholics, who are supposedly weak in will power must give up the little they have if they are to attain sobriety. Listen to this typical alcoholic person as he speaks of his determination and will power.

HE: I admit it—I am an alcoholic but my solution is *just don't drink*. If people urge me to drink, I will refuse it. It is just a matter of not taking that first drink.

I: That sounds like you can lick the problem through your own strength. You feel you can master alcohol with your will power.

HE: I have as much will power as anyone else.

I: You have what you need, then.

HE: Don't you think so?

I: No, not at all.

HE: I don't get it. Doesn't a man have to *try*?

I: You have tried hundreds of times and failed. How many times must you see the evidence?

HE: Hell, I haven't got will power but that is what I need. How do I get it?

I: Your will power is about as useful as trying to remove a mountain by shaking your fist at it.

HE: Yes, but you can shake your fist at the liquor store, the bartender and the people who offer it to you.

I: Fist-shaking and name-calling will not help. Let me explain, John. You began with the idea that you are stronger than your problem. Actually, you are like a man on the Niagara River, headed for the Falls. You still have your oars, however, and you are a strong rower. Slowly your boat is being pulled toward the rapids. Now you row frantically, believing you are strong enough to row to the shore. You still have not faced the truth that the river is more powerful than you. You believe your determination and strength will save you. Let's face it—there are two problems you cannot handle. The one is the Niagara River. The other is alcohol. You have finally met something bigger than you! It is time to abandon all hope in your strength and live only on faith. Will power must die before you are ready to ask for God's power.

The greatest modern experts on the subject of will power are recovered alcoholics. This is what they say:

"The fact is that most alcoholics, for reasons yet obscure, have lost the power of choice in drink. Our so-called will power becomes practically non-existent. We are without defense against the first drink."[1]

"It is when we try to make our will conform with God's that we begin to use it rightly. To all of us, this was a most wonderful revelation. Our whole trouble had been the misuse of will power. We had tried to bombard our problems with it instead of attempting to bring it into agreement with God's intention for us."[2]

The glad news of the Gospel to suffering humanity is this: "Not by might, nor by power, but by my Spirit, says the Lord of hosts" (Zechariah 4:6). To all alcoholics, neurotics, gluttons, homosexuals, addicts, people hooked on power or money or both, sex deviates, psychotics and even tired, weary people like you and me, it can now be said: ENOUGH! *Stop trying—give up the fight—turn off the will power—the battle is over—have faith and be done with your own power!*

Is not this exactly what Paul is urging us to do in Romans and Galatians in the New Testament? It was revealed to Paul that "no man is put right in God's sight because he does what the Law requires; what the Law does is to make man know that he has sinned" (Romans 3:20, Today's English Version). That simply means that will power will not succeed with God. Will power merely brings us to a point where it begins to register with us that our efforts will forever be insufficient. All our frenzied efforts to *do* something only increase the awareness that we are failures.

The Galatians wanted to *do* something—circumcision. Paul says to them in effect: Make up your minds. Either *your* will power or *God's* Power. "You began by God's Spirit; do you now want to finish on your own power?" (Galatians 3:3, TEV). Paul is crystal clear that there is no middle ground where both I-will power and God's power can combine their efforts. "Those who depend on obeying the Law live under a curse.... 'He who is put right with God through faith shall live'" (Galatians 3:10, 11, TEV). ". . . we conclude that a man is put right with God only through faith, and not by doing what the Law commands" (Romans 3:28, TEV).

I wish you could sit as an observor in my study as I bring this message of grace to a hyperactive neurotic person. See how his

---

[1] *Alcoholics Anonymous*, p. 24, AA World Services Inc., Box 459, Grand Central Station, New York, N. Y.

[2] *Twelve Steps and Twelve Traditions*, p. 42, AA World Services, Inc., Box 459, Grand Central Station, New York, N. Y.

hands and feet are in continual motion. His poor mind and heart are working so hard that his blood pressure is at a point where we wonder if this fellow will not soon explode. As he talks, he flits from subject to subject, from problem to problem—always seeking, never finding a solution. We almost weep as we see this man in the bondage of his illness.

Slowly, I get a word in.

"You are so busy, so willing to act. But I have nothing for you to do!"

"You *have* tried and it has not worked. Consider giving up."

"Consider placing one or two of your worries in God's hands. You seem to want to do it all. Let go—let God."

"You are such a fighter. How would you like to find peace?"

"I don't agree with you that it is just a matter of will power. In fact, I suggest you give up what little you have left."

This last comment invariably provokes a reaction to the effect that we must do *something,* that the Lord helps those who help themselves, and that God does not want us to sit still and do nothing.

There is only one sense in which I can agree. We need only surrender. That we can do. But never assault the problem with I-will power. Will power, at best, is like the battery in a car. A good battery will move the car a few feet but it was never intended to carry the passengers any distance. The battery activates the engine which then finds its source of electrical power in its own generator. The generator of an engine cuts out the battery, if I understand automobile mechanics. But perhaps I should stick with the Scriptures which clearly make this point—God's power and man's will power exclude each other, or, if you will, cut each other out as an engine cuts out the power of a battery.

Reliance upon will power is an indication that the will to be omnipotent has not yet died. Caught up in such quixotic dreams, we bite off gargantuan amounts of things needful to us (work, play, sleep, sex, time, etc.); we try to *change* people, fashioning them into what we want them to be; we attempt to alter the unalterable situations of life. We try to do things which God never intended that we do. To surrender these omnipotential urges to God is to finally discover a method of living which will issue in a sense of serene contentment and an authentically human existence. The Serenity Prayer of AA captures this thought:

> God grant me the serenity
> To accept the things I cannot change,

> The courage to change the things I can,
> And the wisdom to know the difference.

The sense of omniscience

Running parallel to the fantasy of the egoist's omnipotence is his sense of omniscience (all-knowing). Again it is an attribute which we strip off from deity and apply to our own persons. The intelligentsia are particularly afflicted with this problem. If one will take the time to sit as a listener to the conversations of pseudo-educated people, he will come away with a number of surprising conclusions.

(1) He will observe that the speaker is almost invariably fascinated with his own thoughts. They delight him. He finds it a pleasure to share them with others. His thoughts seem to shine more brightly than all the others.

(2) He usually holds strongly to the conviction that knowledge (his own first but also others) is potentially capable of solving all problems. There are no limits. No social problem, no marriage problem, no medical problem is unsolvable. All we need is more knowledge, research, study and money to find the solution.

(3) He seldom listens, seldom learns, but is always looking for the opportunity to teach. The idea seems to be to make sure others understand his point. Understanding others is a secondary function which may, at times, serve as a launching pad for the egoist's profundities but the listener is best served by recognizing the exquisite worth of the egoist's brilliance.

I suspect that we are talking about the fundamental reason why most of us become nervous when we are called upon to address a group of people. I have always had a problem in speaking up in groups in which I held no unique or special position. Speaking behind a pulpit has never been a problem because there one speaks upon the invitation of those who listen; moreover, there is time to prepare my remarks.

It is in groups of clergymen—where we are a group of equals—that I have had, until lately, considerable nervousness. Classical and synodical meetings, such as a pastor in the Reformed Church in America is obligated to attend, have always been occasions where I have wanted very much to say something but often could not bring myself to speak, or, saying something, would say it poorly. A few hours of such a meeting would usually make me very depressed.

Why did I react this way among my peers? I had always wanted to think that I just was not equipped for such work; that my early training as a child had gotten me off to a wrong start; that my emotional immaturity stood in the way; that earlier experiences of this kind had so traumatized me that I was unable to cope with these group situations. None of these were true. I was unable to speak in groups until a good friend pointed out to me that most probably, I would not speak in a peer group unless I felt I could say something absolutely brilliant...which I seldom could! Unconsciously, I had laid an egoistic claim upon myself that I needed to say something so intellectually dazzling that it would command the respect and attention of my fellows. Obviously, this was an attempt to "lift" myself to live over and above the *hoi polloi* (the mass of people) whom I needed to see as intellectually inferior. When once I saw this deceptive fantasy and began to say some things to my fellows quite as ordinary as they were saying, running with them the risk of saying something stupid, I was able to speak with far greater comfort and, I trust, good sense.

We all get hung up on this old problem of feeling we know it all. The fantasy of our omniscience is as tragic as it is ludicrous. A few years ago, a recovered alcoholic known only as Allen G., gave an after-dinner speech at an AA banquet which illustrates this human problem unforgettably. This address, so rich in wisdom and good humor, is quoted in full under Appendix A. I encourage you to learn at the feet of this remarkable man who is so much like you and me.

Self-dependency

There is a very strong desire in us for independent, absolutely free, self-originating action. Let us speak of this desire as the *aseity*[3] of man. It would appear that this is another stolen attribute of God.

Consider how difficult it is for us to be dependent on the ideas of others. We much prefer self-originated thoughts. Nothing is so precious to us as an idea which we can call our very own. Second-hand thoughts imply a dependency upon others which is a slur upon our intelligence. Quite honestly, we would often prefer to be wrong with our self-originated ideas than right with the ideas of others. All egoists prize aseity.

If, by the grace of God, a person can begin to accept ideas other than his own, there still remains the problem of *feeling* for the idea. Pastors constantly hear people say things like this: "I know what I should do. I know that I should go to my friend whom I slandered and apologize to him. I was wrong. But I just do not feel I am ready to do it. One has to have the right feeling first. If I

---

[3] Latin: from oneself; self-originating.

went to him and told him I was sorry—why, I would be a hypocrite! I don't *feel* sorry yet. You don't want me to be a hypocrite, do you?"

To that question, I invariably reply "Yes, I want you to be a hypocrite!" That usually shakes up my parishioner sufficiently to become involved in a true dialogue, one in which it is pointed out to him that it is not the danger of hypocrisy which has him hung up, but the reluctance to give up his lingering resentment toward the slandered individual. This resentment is a feeling—*his* feeling. He insists on acting only on his own feelings. So not only is that man under the tyranny of his feelings but, in addition, he obeys only those ideas which he has originated.

There is usually a third and final step by which we establish our aseity. We must originate our thoughts, as we saw. We must also have feeling for any thoughts we desire to put into action. But we feel we must also sovereignly choose the *time* to act. As children, we learn very early to say: "I'll do it when *I* am ready." Not all the powers in heaven and earth can influence our timing. A thing will be done when *we* are ready. Our claim to unconditional independence of action for ourselves is stupendous. We literally aspire to be as self-existent and independently free as the Lord God Himself.

But there is one problem—we *both* cannot possess aseity. Since we deeply and firmly believe in monotheism out of our own emotional needs, we find very little difficulty in understanding that there can really be only one God. Where we get into terrible difficulty is trying to decide who that God will be—the God revealed in Jesus Christ or ourselves.

The veracity of God and man

Let us also look briefly at the veracity of God and how we presumptuously usurp this attribute of God. By veracity, we mean that God is true; that he is free from all falsehood and error; that He is the source of ultimate truth.

I am presently dealing with a man who prides himself in being able to make quick decisions. When I responded by saying he seemed to be an impulsive individual who did a lot of shooting from the hip, he was insulted. "While another man will stand around with his foot in his mouth," I was told, "I make up my mind and *do* something." My parishioner sees this as a mark of strength in himself. I disagree.

It appears to me that he is acting out of weakness when he gives quick answers to all problems. Someone might wish to argue that he does this because he is very insecure and finds some security in a quick decision. This is a good point but let us not overlook my parishioner's unquestioning faith in his capacity to make *right* decisions. He sincerely believes that he is *right* when he makes his decisions and feeling so, he has no need to hesitate to weigh issues. People who could be wrong do that. My parishioner's answer is always right, always true. He is the repository of truth.

This fellow's firm belief in his veracity is reflected in his superstitious way of life. When God has been thrown out of a life, it is understandable that a false theology would immediately rush in to take the place of the Truth. My parishioner has a fantastic collection of superstitious thoughts, all of which he has established as *true*. The signs of the zodiac are carefully studied and the advice of astrologers is accepted with a childlike faith which far exceeds the faith of many Christians. Lucky charms are supposed to have great influence upon his life. All statements about future hopes are invariably accompanied with the sound of knuckles knocking on wood—yes, and the ritual prescribes that it be *only* wood.

What is the meaning of this rank growth of superstition? I suspect it is linked closely to this man's belief in his veracity. Having disposed of God, my parishioner is free—free to state what he thinks is true. All he must do is *think* and it is true. Is not this what God does? With us, once the thought is fashioned and labeled "true," there is no possibility for making a mistake or being in error. I have talked with my parishioner by the hour and have yet to hear one word about his being in error or having made a mistake for which an apology would be in order. No, he is *right,* and he uses all his time with me to defend that position.

Let me add, parenthetically, that if our understanding is correct, the delusion of our veracity would go far in explaining the weird theological systems which are so dear to the adherents of religious sects, not to mention the work published by some of the newest *avant garde* theologians. Are not many of these groups simply building impressive monuments to their conviction that whatever they say is true?

There is, no doubt, a great deal more that could be said about our tendency to attribute divine characteristics to ourselves, but I wish to leave this discussion to make a final point on this matter of playing god. It has to do with our problems with authority. How we relate to authority is, I feel, the most basic problem to which we address ourselves. Will we live in constant fear of it? Do we oppose it? Will we withdraw from it? Or will we become completely servile to authority? Each one of us chooses at least one predominant way to respond to authority. An employee who, when he speaks to his boss, loses his voice, obviously fears authority. A delinquent boy opposes the authority of the police. The student who avoids dialogue with a teacher is withdrawing. Finally, the overcompliant, pious parishioner who can never say "no" to any request that is made of him, is servile to authority.

In our day, we commonly look for the causes of these various responses to authority in our early training. The earliest experiences of children, particularly with their parents, are thought to have a deterministic influence upon the mode of relating to authority in later life. Undoubtedly, some of this is true. But a far more influential factor, I am quite sure, is the manner in which an adult, as an adult, relates himself to the Ultimate Authority, God. I have known a sizeable number of people who had disastrous experiences with authority in childhood, but once finding God and making peace with Him, they have begun to live in a healthy relationship with all authority. I have yet to see a person, maladjusted to authority in his youth, make a healthy adjustment to authority later in life, using only his insight and the "therapeutic relationship" with a human authority-figure to attain this goal. The roots of our authority problem do not appear to be so much in childhood as in the dispute we are currently carrying on with God on the question of who is ultimate—God or us. Once a person enthrones God as the Authority of his life, peace is automatically made with all lesser authority.

7. Law and license

In the year 621 B.C., a high priest in Jerusalem was emptying one of the large collection boxes in the temple area. The "money" in the box was unminted metal, and when it was dumped out, it looked very much like a pile of rusty, scrap metal. As the priest began to sort out the various metals, he came upon an old, dusty scroll, probably in a battered metal box. Someone had thrown it into the collection box perhaps not even aware of the contents.

The priest, being a scholar, could not resist reading a few lines of the scroll. What he read shocked him. He ran to the secretary of King Josiah with the astonishing news: "I have found the book of the law in the house of the Lord" (II Kings 22:8). No time was lost in bringing the scroll to the king, who, when he had read it, rent his clothes in anguish, for what he and his people were doing was quite the opposite of what the law prescribed.

The Book of the Law is what we now know as the Book of Deuteronomy, the Old Testament book which contains the Ten Commandments and a commentary upon it.

No one knew the existence of such a book in the days of King Josiah.

The law of God had been completely forgotten. Incredible!

Meanwhile, the children of Israel, having no laws, walked in their own license.

In modern times, there is scant danger that we will lose the Ten Commandments. Too many copies are printed for that to happen. On this score, therefore, it is doubtful that we will repeat the mistake of the ancient Jews who lost God's law. Yet, in another sense, we today make a mistake quite as serious as the people of Israel. Modern man, in contradiction to the law of God, *constructs his own code of license* without really being aware of his folly. Incredible! We have become ignorant of the fact that each man, if he lives not under the law of God, lives in his own license. One can escape law but he cannot escape license. He may live under one or the other or even under a mutually repellent combination of both, but law and/or license is thrust upon us.

God's law is "given" law, promulgated on the assumption that the world is to function in a theocentric fashion. These laws are explicitly stated in the Ten Commandments, a part of the sacred Scriptures. Man's licenses, however, are self-created guiding principles which nourish and protect man's need to be egocentric. These licenses are hidden many times even to ourselves. We do not like to think of ourselves as having our own private code of ethics.

Let us now look at the Ten Commandments along with our own handcrafted licenses which contradict God's laws.

1.

"Thou shalt have no other gods before me."[1]

Ultimately, there are only two candidates for the position of deity. The God revealed in Jesus Christ is one. The other is man—you, me. You and I may manufacture other deities and worship them, but these are only extensions of ourselves in the world of our fantasies. The candidates remain only two.

This first commandment, therefore, is simply stating that you and I are not allowed to be ultimate. Only the true God can be God. One God.

The man-made license which contradicts the first commandment might read: "I insist upon being ultimate when I so choose." Either God has the last word, or I do. We both cannot have the last word. God claims His right to have it. He will not tolerate a co-deity.

2.

"Thou shalt not make unto thee any graven image...."

This commandment and the third deal with our power needs. The appeal of the graven image was that it was thought to possess power which one could direct and beneficially use in one's life. By creating certain artistic objects, one could, it was thought, control his world the better. The power of the image operated quite apart from God.

We might state our self-authorized license as follows: "My power needs can be met through the things I create." Whenever man turns away from God to the created order and seeks from it the power to live his life—when our dependency is on things rather

---

[1] The Commandments are quoted from the *King James Version* of Exodus 20:1-17.

than God—we are idolatrous. Quite obviously, one look at modern
civilization and it is apparent that much of what man has con-
structed and accomplished is idolatrous. Long ago we finished the
task of making ourselves reasonably comfortable in this old world.
Now we have gone on to raise our towers of Babel and golden
calves. We seek, through the things *we* create, to wield a power
independent from God. That makes us gods.

3.

"Thou shalt not take the name of the Lord thy God in vain...."

We contradict this law when we assert that even sacred and
holy things may be used to establish our personal power and
ultimate position in the world.

King Belshazzar of Babylon, at a feast for a thousand of his
lords, boldly took the sacred vessels which were stolen from the
Temple in Jerusalem and drank wine from them, praising his pagan
deities. This was done to show the king's daring courage, his
boldness, his ultimacy. He liked to do shocking things because it
gave him a reputation for being subject to nothing, save himself.
The bluff worked very well until the handwriting began to appear
on the wall. "Then the king's color changed, and his thoughts
alarmed him; his limbs gave way and his knees knocked together"
(Daniel 5:6). All power left him.

What Belshazzar did with the sacred vessels, we do with cursing, profanity and obscenity. We mean to shock others by such
practices. We wish to impress upon others that we are very strong—
so strong and bold that we can live above the ordinary taboos and
codes to which the masses subject themselves. The sensation of
living above the ordinary religious and social expectations excites
us because we are thereby lifted above the *hoi polloi* (the mass of
people). Thereby we "establish" ourselves as gods, for no matter
how many pious denials we may make, we are then in the position
of deity. Deity is *above* people. Meanwhile, the true God is, quite
frankly, dumped.

4.

"Remember the sabbath day, to keep it holy...."

The fourth commandment deals with our use of time. God has
something to say about how we use our time. We are to rest and
worship one day out of seven. This is for *our* benefit, as are all the
commandments.

We do not like that. Hidden within our hearts is a secret license
which says: "I will order the days of my life as I wish."

And so we do.

Why are we so perverse, even in the face of something which is obviously for our good? If we were at peace with God, we would gratefully comply. The only "benefit" we can possibly extract from our disobedience is the establishment of our own authority—one in opposition to Authority.

5.
"Honour thy father and thy mother...."

Our private code of ethics says something quite different from this command. We reject the implication that we owe honor and respect to parents. We do so on the unconscious assumption that we *owe no man anything.* The very concept of showing honor implies that some glory, some praise, go to another. In the case of parents, it further implies an indebtedness on our part. An egoist sees it as a bother to be obligated to parents. It limits his claim to an unencumbered freedom and detracts from the light of his own glory.

Add to this that our fathers and mothers are authority people. They are a part of a whole framework of authority which includes employers, policemen, pastors, doctors, the FBI and, not least, God. Authority is resented because it is over us; it is stronger than we; authority does not hesitate to impinge upon our freedom; nor does it hesitate to take punitive action against us. For all these reasons, authority is hated.

The violation of the fifth commandment issues in criminal behavior and this is also what the next four commandments speak about—killing, adultery, stealing and lying. A criminal is a person who lives above God's law and works under a code of license of his own construction. The problem is not, it seems to me, that the criminal, in his developmental years, was somehow afflicted with a malformed superego. The criminal mind knows when he is wrong, even though he may either suppress the guilt of his wrongdoing or ignore his guilt while working only under his code of license. A criminal simply does not want to keep the law because that would mean submission to an authority other than his own. His perverse conduct is shaped by being against whatever his authorities are for. In this way, he gets *his* way. His way is a license to be free to do as he wishes.

6.
"Thou shalt not kill."

The authority and power to terminate human life is God's. If we do it, we supersede God.

This commandment, as our Lord interpreted it in Matthew

5:21-26, also brings bad news to our insatiable need to hate. We have built our lives on the premise that *we have a right to be hateful and angry toward whoever we please*—fellow man, God, even ourselves.

The brief sixth commandment sweeps away that treasured right. God tells us to love our enemies, do good to those who persecute us, turn the cheek when we are attacked and pray for our tormentors. Not one of us likes to hear this kind of talk. We see it differently than God. But sooner or later, the issue between God and us must be decided. Either we do it His way or our way. The choice we make in this dilemma determines who is our God. It's really that simple.

7.
"Thou shalt not commit adultery."

The adulterous person says: "My body is mine to use as I wish. I do not wish to be subject to an external law, such as the Seventh Commandment. The law is within me. I am the law and I will do what pleases me and what is right for me—which, in my book is the same thing."[2]

8.
"Thou shalt not steal."

The license of man says: "What I need, I take."

9.
"Thou shalt not bear false witness against thy neighbour."

We say: "The protection of my own skin and the advancement of my own cause are more important than the needs and rights of others."

10.
"Thou shalt not covet...."

We say: "I have a perfect right to be discontented with what I have ... and to do something about it."

The enthroned egoist, working on the assumption that he is ultimate, leaves God's laws and lives in a state of license. He often does this unawares—not realizing that he makes himself his own highest power, nor that he is setting up his own code of ethics against the Almighty's. Many people, when this is disclosed to

---

[2] For an extended discussion, see the author's book, *Search for Identity,* Grand Rapids: Zondervan, 1967, Chapter 26, "Sexual Relationships Outside of Marriage."

them, complain that this is an unfair judgment. If a true picture were drawn, we are assured, it would reveal that we have walked humbly all the days of our years; that we have never tried to be ultimate; that we have tried to keep the law of God, albeit not always with success; that we really do approve of God and we sincerely hope He approves of us. We have always considered ourselves to be fundamentally religious and if we tally up the sum total of what we have done, we feel that our virtues will shine brightly. As for our sins, they were honest mistakes. Aside from the suspiciously defensive tone of our protestations, we ought to notice that (1) the egoist is unaware of his ultimacy as well as his egocentric license, yet he lives his life on the basis of it, while (2) he is consciously aware of God and His laws but rebels against them at his choosing. On both scores, man is in rebellion against God.

Accepting responsibility for what we have done amiss is surely a first and needful step out of the darkness of sin into which we have plunged ourselves. It is deeply disturbing to come to realize that our malfunctioning lives are of our own creation; that our mistakes were *our* mistakes; that what we are now reaping is only what we have earlier sown. Necessary and beneficial though this is, however, it is only the beginning of a solution to our problems.

Not until one begins to see himself in the light of God's law, can one have the beginning of an awareness that one has done something *wrong*. Paul says: ". . . what the law does is to make man know that he has sinned" (Romans 3:20, TEV). The law of God is a mirror in which we are at last able to see ourselves as we truly are ". . . if it had not been for the law, I should not have recognized sin *or* have known its meaning. [For instance] I would not have known about covetousness—would have had no consciousness of sin or sense of guilt—if the Law had not [repeatedly] said, You shall not covet. . ." (Romans 7:7, *The Amplified Bible*). What is true of coveting would hold for any of the commandments of God.

As a pastor, I have come upon a few people who were as ignorant as was King Josiah of God's laws, but such cases are rare. Yet, there are people who are only vaguely aware that it is wrong to commit adultery, to steal, to lie, etc. It is news to them that God has spoken against such deeds. As King Josiah was overcome with a sense of guilt on hearing God's law, so are some today smitten in their consciences when first they read the law of God.

Admittedly, it is only a very small percentage of people in our Christian culture who are truly ignorant of God's law. Most people know it and ignore it; or, taking it somewhat seriously, they feel that it does not touch them. As people read it superficially, they feel that they are not especially guilty of anything, but if they are, there are understandable reasons for doing what they did.

I can clearly recall how, as a boy, I would listen to my pastor read the law each Sunday morning. It was for me one of the more satisfying parts of the worship service. As the pastor would read each commandment, I would silently check off each one with the thought, "Okay, as far as that one goes!" By the time all ten were read, I was bathing myself in sanctity. My deluded pharisaism was made possible, of course, by not going too far with the intent of each commandment. Had I interpreted the commandments as Christ explained them in the Sermon on the Mount, I would have been spared the painful suffering which is always the cost of that easy virtue which is no virtue at all.

Many people, even when confronted with God's law, are not smitten with a sense of guilt. Unless that happens, how will people ever come to a realization of their estrangement from God? How will they ever come to know their sin? Until the fact of sin and guilt is established in a person, there is obviously no need for Jesus Christ, "the Lamb of God, who takes away the sin of the world" (John 1:29). Salvation presupposes an acknowledged despair over sin. How can one be saved if he does not understand that he is a sinner, guilty in the eyes of God's law?

Notice, however, that there is something wrong with these questions. They all possess an undeclared intent to somehow make a person feel guilty. Yet, no one has ever experienced a sense of guilt simply by another accusing him of wrong doing. That is exactly what we do when we crudely use the law of God as an instrument to make people feel guilty. Not even God accuses us. One's conscience may accuse himself (Romans 2:15) but this is something quite different than an accusation from outside ourselves which seeks to batter us into a state of guilty submission.

Rather than an accusatory approach, what is needed, it would seem, is a personalized portrayal of one's own licenses in all of their folly. One can point out in his own personal life how we have issued ourselves a fantastic set of licenses each of which flies in the face of God's laws. Let me quickly give an example.

In the course of a conversation, a man said to me: "Nobody but nobody is going to tell *me* what to do. I always make my own decisions." We need not even know the context of these remarks to understand that the man felt he was ultimate in the world. It would have been folly to appraise the man that he was a lawbreaker, violating the first commandment ("Thou shalt have no other gods before me.") But it was eventually helpful to him when I gently pointed out that he sounded very much like me when I was my highest power. I went on to describe the string of problems which plagued me when I was not yet under new management. At this, he pricked up his ears and asked questions. I answered them by talking about *my* tendency to be ultimate but even more, about that new Manager. Soon my friend was able to see in me the thing which was plaguing his life and by that time, the three of us—God, he and I—were in a most helpful dialogue. I sensed the birth of hope in this man when it was time to part.

The most helpful and telling thing we can do for a fellow traveler through life, is to share with him our own delusions and shortcomings. This disarms a person. Defense is then unnecessary. The listener can safely relax sufficiently to give an empathetic ear to the plight of the other person. There is usually enough sadism in us to even enjoy the account of another's personal disaster. One may then, hopefully, begin to pick up interest as he finds a correspondence between this person's problem and his own. The next step is crucial—it is to live vicariously into another's problems. Many, when they later emerge from such a dialogue are ready to say—"We are the same! His problems are mine. We are in this together. I was as mixed-up, frustrated and as *wrong* as he!"

At such a point, one often experiences an overwhelming sense of guilt. We ought now to talk about guilt. In the chapter following, let us look particularly at the various ways in which we attempt to deal with guilt.

8. The action of guilt

> . . . the Lord . . . redeems your life from the Pit. . .
> PSALM 103:3, 4.

The Pit—what is that? It is the point where a drug addict finds himself after years of addiction; it is the place at which the devotees of sex find themselves when their perverted minds lose all desire for genuine love; it is the tragedy of repetitive lawlessness in the life of a criminal which eventually leads him to a prison cell.

There is a power of destruction at work in each one of these people, for they are breaking themselves down. They are destroying themselves.

This power of destruction is at work within us all to varying degrees. Perhaps we have learned to shield it from others with a great deal of sophistication but the destroyer is in every heart. Let us construct a model to illustrate this mysterious power of destruction which is strong enough to lead us into the Pit.

Saul Kish is a handsome young man in his mid-thirties. He is married and has four children. Saul is active in scouting, the Lions, the PTA and the volunteer ambulance squad. Everyone knows him as a respected, capable leader in his community. Mr. Kish is a salesman who earns a very comfortable living. He attends church occasionally and would like to be more faithful were it not for a strange, uncontrollable impulse to weep during the service.

This urge to cry puzzled me until I learned about what Saul calls his "path of devastation." For some time he has had a paramour and she is now pregnant. He has also had an alcohol problem which is now coming out into the open. In addition, Saul has had problems with his employers, of whom he has had three new ones this past year. Under the weight of all these crosses, it is ironic that Saul is afflicted with back trouble and underwent surgery three months ago. Small wonder that with so much devastation and destruction in his life, Saul weeps tears of compassion for himself during moments of reflection in worship.

It is obvious that this "path of devastation" is the result of a terribly destructive force in Saul's life. There are all kinds of fancy labels which we moderns use to designate this destructive, alien force in a person, but no matter what we call it, it always boils down to the same word—sin. Sin is the violation of God's ordering of life. When His laws are transgressed, sin is committed, and, the wages of sin is death, as Paul says. Many people spurn these simple, unalterable realities, complaining that the terms are meaningless and the ideas questionable. Strange, but as a working pastor, I have come to believe more each day in the Biblical analysis of the cause of destructiveness in people. Sin is a reality with which we must deal.

But how does sin cause all this destruction in our lives? The answer lies in what sin inevitably produces—a sense of guilt. What we see in Saul is the action of guilt which, no doubt, has slowly accumulated through the years and now is mushrooming with explosive violence in his conduct. We know that guilt is the culprit because it is the only human feeling which prompts a person to become *self*-accusatory and *self*-destructive. Once an individual points his finger at his own guilt, he will either work on self-atonement devices (which never work) or he goes to Christ, confessing his sins and trusting our Lord's atonement.

I have never heard of a better description of guilt than that it is a "damning feeling." Precisely. It is no wonder, therefore, that we naturally seek to rid ourselves of it. Let us look at our major self-atonement devices. We humans attempt to do this in at least four different ways, none of which work.

(1) The most common device is the mask of virtue. Saul is an expert at this with his pseudo-piety. Few scout masters have done as much for their boys as had Saul. Mothers and fathers of the scouts wrote letters of appreciation, calling him a Pied Piper. The ambulance squad lavished praise and honor on Saul for his outstanding dedication. When Saul was sober, his wife boasted of him as an ideal husband and father. Frankly, almost everyone was taken in, as we say, with the good works of this bright, young man. People would say: "Saul Kish has many faults but as many virtues. It pretty well evens out."

That is exactly what Saul wanted people to say. When they said it, they fell into the very same error as Saul. He is a master at balancing his debauched life with just enough piety to muffle his screaming conscience. He uses piety to deal with his guilt. Saul is attempting self-atonement. His "goodness" is supposed to compensate for his life of adultery, alcoholism and the destruction of his family. The strategy, unfortunately, never works.

(2) Another self-atonement device is to destroy the law. This is the way of the criminal and Saul has some of this in him. He contemptuously flaunts the law of marriage. To use another example, the doctor who operated on his back laid down the law to Saul concerning physical exertion, but within two weeks, Saul was out fishing in a rocking rowboat. Saul, moreover, seems to possess a special faculty for telling convincing lies.

What better news for a guilty man than the fantasy that laws do not really exist, or, if they do, that they may be broken with impunity. If people are hurt by what one does, reasons the criminal, they deserve it. The lawbreaker is always justified in his own eyes while society and its laws are wrong. All this to cover that unrelenting, damning sense of guilt.

(3) We observe also this about Saul—he is physically ill. He has chronic back trouble and, as a result of his alcoholism, the beginning of cirrhosis and minor brain deterioration.

Do we actually mean to say that Saul Kish has these illnesses because he is a greater sinner than other men? No, he is no greater sinner, I am sure, than you and I. We all stand equally guilty before the Judgment Seat of God. But most assuredly I mean to say that there is a connection between guilt and physical illness. The latter is a do-it-yourself method of guilt disposal. "Is any among you sick?" asks James, "... confess your sins to one another, and pray for one another, that you may be healed" (James 5:14, 16). To the paralytic man at Bethzatha, Jesus said: "See, you are well! Sin no more, that nothing worse befall you" (John 5:14). The paralytic at Capernaum was addressed similarly: "Take heart, my son, your sins are forgiven" (Matthew 9:2).

(4) There is, finally, the self-atonement device of emotional illness. Our feelings can become ill just as do our bodies. When one is emotionally ill, we say he suffers from a neurosis or a psychosis. Can there be any crueler form of self-destruction? Not one of us would inflict such a punishment on his worst enemy, but as we live with our personal guilt which cries out continually for atonement, we feel that the curse of insanity would be a light verdict for the guilt that resides in us. O. Hobart Mowrer, in a remarkable book entitled *The Crisis in Psychiatry and Religion* (Princeton: Van Nostrand, 1961) has presented, from a psychological point of view, the relationship between guilt and mental illness. Dr. Mowrer has dealt with considerable clinical data and uncovered many insights which are a confirmation of the scriptural position that sin and its consequence, guilt, is the key human problem.

Thank God that Saul Kish did not travel the road to mental

illness in his unsuccessful search for atonement. Indeed, none of these self-atonement devices are effective. They do nothing to cleanse our guilty consciences. They only increase our despair and bondage. There is no *human* way in which to effectively deal with the problem of guilt.

More needs to be said about the *bondage* of sin and guilt in emotional illness and to this matter we now address ourselves.

9. The life of bondage

The dearest word in the vocabulary of the self-enthroned egoist is *freedom*.

The egoist desires to act as he pleases, at the time of his choosing, in the manner which best suits him.

He does not want people telling him what to do.

He detests working under the authority-structures of society. They fence him in and limit his freedom.

The best time of the week for a man intoxicated with this kind of freedom is Friday evening as he rides alone down an open highway with a full wallet to a destination of his choosing. He then feels free from a boss who can tell him what to do: free to travel any road he wishes; free to spend some money (he will determine the amount) on anything he wishes to buy; free to go to a city of his selection. As he speeds down the highway, he says to himself: "This is the life. I am now free to do as I wish."

It is possible for a freedom-obsessed person to establish this attitude as a way of life. It then becomes a passion which recurrently grips him. The desire to be free, to live without a lid on his life, binds him. He is really in bondage to himself because, by casting off all control over him, he has become his own lord and master. God accepts such a decision, defers to it and accepts a secondary position in this person's world. There is then no more need for faith in God because it is believed He is only a secondary power. Now we can understand Paul as he says: ". . . whatever does not proceed from faith is sin" (Romans 14:23).

Sin, therefore, not only issues in that destructive guilt which we examined in a preceding chapter, but also in bondage. Our Lord said: "Truly, truly, I say to you, every one who commits sin is a slave to sin" (John 8:34). The speaker of these words of truth understood that the human problem is simply that we are bound people. We are slaves under the bondage of sin.

Let us try to form a clear image of a person who is in this bondage of which we speak. I think of him simply as a person who cannot begin when he wishes to begin and who cannot stop when he wishes to stop. In a moment, we will see numerous examples of this. A free person, on the other hand, is one who can begin and stop at his choosing. When he wishes to do something, he is able to bring himself to do it. He does it freely. And when he wishes to stop doing whatever he is doing, he feels no compulsion to continue. Paul in Romans 7 explains that the inability to begin and cease is precisely the problem of all who are enslaved to sin. In such a bondage, we cry out: "I can will what is right, but I cannot do it. For I do not do the good I want, but the evil I do not want is what I do" (verses 18, 19).

These words clearly describe a person in bondage. The bondage we are talking about here is precisely what we see in the varying forms of emotional illness. Emotional illness is a modern way of describing what in New Testament days was called the bondage of sin. Once we come to understand that emotional illness is fundamentally a problem of the controls in a person not functioning properly—that is, he has lost the freedom to begin and to cease— then we today may be ready to listen with more attentiveness to Christ the Healer who made this promise: ". . . if the Son makes you free, you will be free indeed" (John 8:36).

Our inability to begin

Let us mention some random illustrations of our "unfreedom" to begin doing something even though we want very much to do it.

Some of us desire, but yet are not free, to make certain verbal statements when it is appropriate to do so. I think of several individuals who find it impossible to say to their spouses: "I love you." They *want* to say it, but never do. The words stick in their throats. The same is true of the words: "I am sorry. I apologize." One is surprised at the number of people who have never in their lives apologized to an offended party. It is not because an apology is thought to be unnecessary. This person believes he should apologize but he is blocked—he never does it. He cannot bring himself to do it.

Another instance of such bondage is the person who cannot speak up in a group. Yesterday a man pleaded with me never to call on him for a reaction in the group in which he is a member. I asked if he *wanted* to speak. He did! But if I would call on him, he would get up and walk out because "I just cannot bring myself to do it." This reaction is parallel to certain parishioners who find it impossible to pray aloud in a group. It is amazing to see someone in a small group happily chatting and talking without interruption for a full hour, suddenly freeze in terror as the pastor turns to him with a request that he offer prayer. "I'll come to the meeting, Reverend, but I just cannot offer prayer!" I understand, particularly in the case of prayer, for the word which sticks most in our throats and is most difficult to speak reverently, is the word *God*. We like to talk about Him but cannot address Him by name. We have locked jaws because we are locked people.

Think of the ways in which we are in bondage when it comes to the use of our time. Habitual procrastination is a good example. The person who continually puts things off until he is coerced into doing what is expected of him, is not a free person. Such is the person who cannot get up in the morning. On retiring, he announces to his wife his sincere intention of rising at an early hour. The wife, knowing his pattern, expresses her doubts but is reassured that "this time it will be different." But with this particular kind of person and problem, it never is. He desires but cannot do what he wishes to do. Just as his wife, who is forever late in her appointments with her husband desires to be on time, but never is. She resolves to change. She hates to be late. She is sure that she can be different. Her waiting husband, however, knows that the promise will not be kept. Not until his wife becomes a free person will she be able to manage the use of her time.

What we have mentioned to this point might be called low-order examples of neurotic behavior. There are more painful examples of our difficulty with beginning, such as sexual impotence in a male and frigidity in a female. Almost every person I have encountered with such a problem has desired a full and satisfying sexual life. What they really want, they are denied by their uncooperative bodies. They are not free to begin love play though desiring it. Imagine the suffering in this kind of bondage!

In our day, the commonly accepted explanation of frigidity and impotence in people who desire sexual fulfillment is that they are troubled by long-standing unconscious factors which must be resolved before the person can again be sexually healthy. It is the psychiatrist to whom the sufferer turns with these psycho-sexual disorders. Thank God that there is usually some amelioration of the problem in the hands of our medical people. It is questionable, however, whether a deep and lasting healing takes place through the therapeutic efforts of the psychotherapist. Later, in Chapter 11, a reason will be offered from a religious point of view for the undeniable measure of healing that takes place. At this point, however, I raise the question whether it is really necessary to introduce the idea of the unconscious mind as an avenue through which healing is to take place. From a pastoral viewpoint, it is sufficient to see the frigid woman and the impotent man as locked people, as people who are in bondage.

Of course, everything depends now on whether the Christian faith can *really* show us the way to lasting, inner freedom. I deeply believe God has shown us the way to such a freedom. Our Lord, as He began His ministry, promised us freedom in these words: "He has sent me to proclaim release to the captives and recovering of sight to the blind, to set at liberty those who are oppressed . . ." (Luke 4:18). The truth of these words has been confirmed in the hearts of countless Christians who have really been born into the kingdom of God. How one obtains Christ's freedom will be discussed in the remaining chapters. But let us now return to a few more examples of human bondage.

The inability to begin doing what one has chosen to do is clearly demonstrated in the phobic attacks and anxiety reactions which one commonly sees in neurotic people. Our fears and anxiety may cripple us to such an extent that we become absolutely paralyzed. In such a state we can do nothing. Our friends must care for us, sometimes for a long period. This sense of dread and fear may also be of short duration. I recall once worshiping in a church where the pastor, quite unexpectedly, called on me to pronounce the benediction. I was honored by this request and gladly came forward from my seat in the congregation. As I came to the pulpit, I was unaccountably seized with anxiety. The blood seemed to rush out of my head; my heart was pounding; worst of all, I could not recall the words of the benediction! I paused, sweating. The people were standing, waiting. I quickly decided to compose a new benediction—which I am sure no one understood and to this day is beyond my recall—only to turn into a new problem: my voice was quaking and cracking. A short time later I was perfectly all right again, but I had momentarily experienced the anxiety which a more neurotic person experiences almost continuously. My anxiety attack was such, however, that it prohibited me from doing what I really wanted to do.

Before leaving this matter of problems in beginning, I wish to cite an illness which the older psychiatrists called neurasthenia. "Neurasthenia is an old term which is often still used to describe people who are tired, depressed, lackadaisical, slightly irritable, and who cannot concentrate on anything and like to lie around without much responsibility."[1] Anyone who thinks neurasthenic

---

[1] Eric Berne, *A Layman's Guide to Psychiatry and Psychoanalysis*, New York: Simon and Schuster, 1957, p. 152.

people really like to be that way do not, it seems to me, understand these people. They sincerely desire to be active, responsible and energetic. We should accept their honesty and frankness when they tell us that they just cannot bring themselves to act this way. They really cannot because they are in bondage. They have lost the freedom to do the thing they really wish to do. With Paul they cry out: "What an unhappy man I am! Who will rescue me from this body that is taking me to death?" (Romans 7:24 TEV). But not even this earnest cry rouses them from the couch on which they spend twenty hours a day. You can see here that we have not only a problem of beginning but also of stopping. Let us now consider this aspect of the problem.

Our inability to stop

We are discussing the problem of control in the human person. Emotional illness is simply a name to describe what happens to a person out of control. If the controls are working well, we say the person is healthy. We have, to this point, talked about people who have difficulty in controling themselves sufficiently to begin doing things. The problem of control is quite as acute in stopping what we have begun. On these two "hooks"—the problem of beginning and the problem of stopping—we can hang most every emotional illness, the neuroses as well as the psychoses.

One of the most common and understandable examples of our inability to stop is seen in our tendency to worry. We have already seen that worry is a sign of mispositioning because our time-bite becomes inappropriately enlarged. Worse, we grab the controls of our lives and begin pushing all the buttons, if not by our deeds, then at least in our minds. Worry indicates that we have jumped out of the human category and established ourselves among the gods. Admittedly, there is a kind of happy exultation in the early stages of worry. We feel a kind of challenge in the problem-solving aspects of that about which we are worried. In addition, we are deeply committed to the idea that *we* can think our way out of tough situations, thereby avoiding to bother the Almighty. To this point, we seem to enjoy our worry, at least until we wish to stop our worry machinery. Then to our consternation, we find we cannot shut the works down! We *can't* stop worrying!

The hypochondriac is a good illustration. Some of us have such an inordinate concern about our health that to other "normal" people we look, and indeed are, quite ridiculous. We run to the doctor with each ache and pain. If we are too "ill" to see the doctors we manipulate others to run to him for us. We bathe ourselves in self-concern and dry ourselves in the warmth of self-pity. Even if such people are persuaded to seek psychiatric help, the prognosis is very poor.

And yet, the problem is, in a certain sense, very simple. All we need do is help this person stop worrying about his body, assuming, of course, that he wishes to be helped. Naturally, where there is no faith, no desire to become well, there will be no healing, as Jesus taught us. It is a fact, however, that hidden in even the most crippled neurotic is some desire to become well. There is undoubtedly a contradictory attitude, perhaps of greater strength, which does not desire good health, but this does not invalidate the presence of a genuine desire to halt one's hypochondriacal tendencies. We simply do not listen today to the worrywart, the alcoholic, the insomniac, the compulsive masturbator, the glutton, the hypochondriac, and the list could go on, when they tell us they *want to quit.* They really do. We *should* believe them. They are right. But their problem is that they are locked, bound up, shackled. They cannot do what they really wish to do. It is a state of unfreedom.

The way out for the hypochondriac, someone might suggest, is to bring his desire to be well to a point where it slightly exceeds his desire to remain sick. I think such would be the goal of many present-day counselors. They would encourage the sick person to satisfy himself with having a slight edge of victory in the war which must go on without termination. But this is not healing in the Christian sense. The healing which Christ gives is the result of the end of the war between "I would like to ..." and "I do not want to . . ." Christ does not offer superficial health, nor pseudo-freedom ". . . if the Son makes you free, you will be free indeed" (John 8:36).

Another person who has terrible difficulties stopping is the drug addict. There was a day when he could take the drug and then cease taking it. That was when he first began. Soon thereafter, at a point of time of which the drug addict was totally unaware, he became hooked. He became an addict—physically, psychologically, but most of all spiritually, for he lost his freedom. Thereafter, he lives under the tyranny of his feelings. This person, a human spirit, is locked in the prison house of his lower nature—that nature of emotionality which we share with animals. Put a little differently, we could say that the choice-making machinery is locked up.

As a result, he is incapable of making a direct decision with regard to drugs but he is able to make a decision which will indirectly help him to become drug-free. Concretely, the drug addict cannot be expected to choose against heroin, but he surely is able to make a decision to unreservedly seek the help of a group such as Narcotics Anonymous.

We have already alluded in passing to three other problems which ultimately boil down to a problem in stopping—alcoholism, insomnia and gluttony. Again, these problems occur in people who really do wish to stop doing what they are doing. Somewhere in each compulsive eater, for example, is a desire to stop. That desire may be small, momentary and pushed aside by a hundred other desires, but it is there. The gluttonous person does not really wish to gorge himself. No one decides on a certain day of his life that he wants to become overweight. Indeed, this is the very thing which the person does not want. True, he flatly refuses to pay the price which must be paid if he is to maintain a proper weight, but this is not because he is a depraved person but because he *cannot* stop.

Some may say that the compulsive eater is weak-willed, ineffective, even shiftless. Happily, Christ took a more compassionate view of such people. He sees us as sincerely wanting, but not being able to stop. Were the Lord here today, He might use the illustration of a toboggan ride. The problems of stopping are akin to stopping a toboggan. For what can one do to stop the toboggan once it is halfway down the mountain? Nothing. No amount of determination or will power can help. If one drags his hands, he will fall off. If he drags his feet, he will hurt himself. Toboggans have no brakes. They cannot be stopped.

Perhaps this illustration of a descending toboggan can help us to see another irrational aspect in this problem of stopping. Our problem is not only that we try, usually by means of brute strength to stop the toboggan when it is halfway down the mountain, but even worse, once it comes to rest we go right back up the mountain and repeat the very same thing. We now become compulsive about the toboggan. It *must* be stopped. We will try again and again until we succeed—which never happens.

Our compulsions, it would seem, are our most eloquent expressions of unfreedom, of our bondage. We feel out of control in a compulsion, unable to stop, though we sincerely wish to stop. We are inexorably drawn to do what we wish we would not do. The tragedy of this kind of life is dramatically illustrated in the life of Elizabeth Burns (a pseudonym) a millionaire's daughter who was alcoholic, a drug addict, suicidal and thrice-married. She writes: "Aware that what I was doing was beyond decency, it seems I had to do it, *had* to just as I had to guzzle, hating both, hating me, yet having to. A strange strange war between two selves, the one self running headlong, faster, ever faster; the other alongside, crying out, abusing, warning, pointing to the finish."[2]

The more tragic forms of compulsion can be seen in suicide and homicide. Suicide is the consequence of not being able to stop. Perhaps long ago, the thought of self-annihilation was only a thought, but somehow it was nursed along until, without knowing it, the person has become "hooked" on the thought. The idea seems to have a strange fascination and appeal, even though in his better moments, he wants to live. But the idea of suicide persists, secretly. He now feels strangely drawn to the act. At this time, he already begins to drop veiled hints of what he plans to do and not far off is the explicit statement of his plan and a time to carry it out. This is why the suicidal person is so difficult for us to understand—he is so methodical and calculating in a thing which he really does not wish to do, but is doing because he is not free to stop. He seems to reach a point of no return where his controls no longer function.

Stopping is also the problem encountered in homicide. The volcanic hatred in a person may finally burst through into actions so explosive that they cannot be contained. It is a fact that most murders are committed by noncriminals, ordinary citizens who would never normally set out with the intention of actually committing murder, but who "got out of hand" and "went too far," to the amazement of everyone including themselves.

We see out-of-control people most clearly, perhaps, in the increasingly prevelant mass murders by people who are said to be criminally insane. In 1966, Charles Whitman of Austin, Texas killed 13 people and wounded 31 in an orgy which gives us a most bizarre example of a person out of control. Five months before ascending the University of Texas tower from which he shot his victims, Whitman told a psychiatrist that he was making "intense efforts" to control his temper, but he was worried that he might explode. Already at the time of his visit to his doctor, Whitman was thinking about "going up on the tower with a deer rifle and start shooting people." Family problems and academic concerns continued to exert heavy pressure on Whitman (an engineering student) until he seemed to reach a point of controlled controllessness. With deliberation and well-calculated plans, Whitman proceeded to murder his victims, picking them off one by one from the tower. He was stopped only when the police gunned him down, for Charles Whitman could not stop himself.

---

[2] Elizabeth Burns, *The Late Liz,* New York: Appleton-Century-Croft, 1957, p. 61.

We have given at some length various examples of human bondage. This bondage is both a sense of being driven when one does not wish to begin and a sense of out-of-controlness when one wishes to cease. Many more examples could be given of this basic problem in us. I am tempted to illustrate how it can be seen, for example, in the way we really do not wish to become resentful, but yet continue our resentments even while we desire to cease from them. The same can be seen in our problems with continual jealousy, adamant unteachableness, ceaseless marital conflict, an obsession with power, a continuing fascination with violence, driving compulsions, recurrent lawlessness, recurrent moods of depression, repetitive bizarre fantasies, ceaseless running from problems, money madness, alcoholism, compulsive religiosity, compulsive speaking, etc.—only God knows the number of things on which we can become hooked. When one is hooked, he is not free.

In summary, we have tried to discern the element of bondage in the human person. Little was said as to the dynamics of how this bondage becomes established in the life of each person. Our Lord taught us that "everyone who commits sin is a slave to sin" (John 8:34). Sin, but perhaps more particularly the guilt which issues from it, is the cause of this bondage. Beyond this, however, we need not speculate since it is academic for our purposes.

It is sufficient to recognize this bondage as it comes to concrete expression in our lives. Since bondage was defined as the inability to begin or cease at will, an attempt was made to view the various kinds of emotional illness from this point of view. No attempt was made to be exhaustive but enough material was presented, it is hoped, to suggest that bondage is the constant element in the various types of emotional disorder.

We are now ready to deal with the way in which God gives us freedom from our bondage and to that happy task we now turn to Part III.

PART III

Life Through Death

10. The way of the cross

If we are really going to communicate in these last chapters, it will be helpful if I become somewhat autobiographical. I wish to share with you some experiences out of which my perspective has been shaped. No man can avoid coming out of a certain unique kind of context. Indeed, the God of our lives so shapes our backgrounds and creates our individual histories as to effectively bring us to a better knowledge of His ways and His truth.

Religiously, I was raised in a strongly conservative branch of the Reformed tradition. I knew very early in life "how great my sins and miseries are," to quote the Heidelberg Catechism. I understood also that my faith was weak and that much was lacking in my prayer life. It grieved me that I knew so little of the Bible. I sincerely felt that I was a very poor Christian in spite of my best efforts, and I learned to accept my sinful depravity. Please do not infer from this any criticism of my religous heritage. I respect and honor the Reformed faith as I do my parents who taught it to me. The problem was not with my heritage nor my parents, but with myself for not perceiving what my heritage was really saying.

What I would like you to observe about my religious life at this point is that I saw myself as small, diminished, underdeveloped and helpless. It was my childish, distorted view of man. A child naturally wants to see himself as a child and it is understandable that he will strongly believe in those parts of his religious heritage which reinforce the child-image in him. Children, because they are born with a tendency toward self-centeredness, pass by most of the religious teaching which does nothing for their self-image.

Much later, in my theological studies, I took a good, hard look at the more liberal, socially-oriented forms of Protestant Christianity. They tantalized and impressed me for a time. As I see it now, my slight affair with liberalism was possible because it also sees man as small, broken and helpless—albeit, with potential strength to lift himself. Religious liberalism calls people to an evolutionary ascent, to the growth of one's person and character from something embryonic to full maturation. But again, the starting point is man as he appears through the wrong end of a telescope.

Still later, I encountered the world of psychology and psychiatry. The world of Freud and his followers was like wine and I soon became intoxicated. I now had *answers*. It was a dazzling, promising world. Looking back, I was fascinated with it partly, I suppose, because it left my view of man undisturbed; partly because I saw hope of helping myself and others to human wholeness through its techniques and methods.

I said the world of mental science left my view of man (as despicable and small) undisturbed. As a psychiatrically oriented pastor, I saw man as thinking too little of himself. Man, I felt, should be viewed not as a prideful person who commits sin but rather as a person who lacks ego strength. In fact, he is so weak that no real connection can be drawn between sin and mental illness.[1] Man's problem is his immaturity, I argued. He is too self-despising and as a result, feels unwarranted guilt. Man's problem was also that he did not sufficiently love himself. I saw man as "the broken child"—broken by an often cruel heredity, by faulty training in the formative years, by the destructive influence of a bad environment and an inability to properly love himself. These were the culprits which were causing mental illness in people, to my way of thinking.

So I set out to slay these culprits which were causing all this malfunction in people. I saw no reason—I was so logical (and omnipotent!)—why a well-trained counselor, working with a co-operative counselee, should not be able to know the factors of human illness, control them and eventually eliminate them. Man could solve his emotional problems with the latest and best knowledge, with determined will power and with practiced skill. To be sure, we needed God to help us but only in the sense that "God helps those who help themselves." God makes *us* strong to save. It was magical thinking, I argued, to literally believe that "*God* is our strength."

Once again, I felt that what man needed most of all was merely to grow to a point where he could really affirm and respect himself as a worthy person. One might gradually grow into a

---

[1] The modern mood, of course, is to see mental illness as simply a sickness. In an enlightening chapter entitled " 'Sin,' the Lesser of Two Evils" (Chapter 4) in *The Crisis in Psychiatry and Religion*, O. Hobart Mowrer explodes the "sickness theory" and argues convincingly that the roots of the problem are found in sin.

mature, loving person if he were provided with a therapeutic relationship created by a counselor who had good psychological training. A good therapist would help the thwarted child in us out of his confinement, setting him free at last to grow.

Looking back, I now understand why I hung on so tenaciously to this view of the "thwarted child." As long as I could see myself and others in this light, it would be unnecessary to deal with the gigantic amounts of pride in my heart created by my "I-am-a-god" image. For how can you say to an adult who is seen as a thwarted child, "Your style of life is basically egocentric?" How can you confront an adultish child with a moral standard when all he is doing is trying his best to grow up? What the thwarted child needed, I felt, was encouragement to grow, to live, to mature—surely not an invitation to die to his egocentricity, to surrender to God's terms, and to repent of his sin against God's Laws. It is no wonder, therefore, that the way of the cross—the cross being the symbol of the way by which God tells us that *His* terms are the death of my pride and egoism—meant little to me.

I would have remained in this delusion had not the Lord introduced me to some truly remarkable people. They were some recovered alcoholics from Alcoholics Anonymous. At first they baffled and annoyed me because they did not fit into my neat analysis of what makes people tick. But then my eyes began to open. What struck me about these AA people was that these were *transformed* people who followed a program in which God was the most important part. The first step of their program was to admit defeat, surrender to God and turn oneself over to a Higher Power—a power even higher than the exalted heights of the alcoholic's egoism. They insisted that the alcoholic come to *God's* terms, which meant that the alcoholic, probably for the first time in his life would not have life the way *he* wanted it. Also, the alcoholic was encouraged to make a full, honest, moral inventory in the presence of God and a third party. At first I was highly skeptical of AA's approach but as I studied those who seriously undertook this program, it became apparent that these people were years ahead of me in the understanding of human problems.

I decided to become a student and sit at the feet of these "drunks and bums of A.A.," as they sometimes laughingly call themselves. They taught me many strange things, but what shook me up most was the discovery that AA would have nothing to do with my concept of "the broken child." Man was seen first of all as "playing god." These AA people talked a lot about pride, phoniness, false ego, the big head and the high horse. And not only that! They also had the audacity to *tell* a man when he was indulging himself in such luxuries as self-pity, "stinkin' thinkin'," resentment and self-deception, to mention just a few favorite topics. It was soon apparent to me that AA viewed man as an arrogant giant rather than a victimized child. But was AA right?

I was desperate for an answer and remember this period of my life as a time of agony. Almost all my cherished ways of thinking were being upset. In my pain, I turned to the Scriptures for guidance and to God for an answer. He answered me not with a particular verse of Scripture, nor with some kind of intuitive revelation but with a new way of reading the Scriptures. My slant changed. The Book looked different, read differently than it ever had before. I began to understand its perspective. Now I could see from Genesis to Revelation that man in his sinful condition is prideful—or to put it more modernly, the Bible depicts man's basic problem as egocentricity.

My way of "reading" life itself changed. It was now possible to see in the lives of others this prideful way of living. For example, a woman related to me that she went to her pastor and complained that she was terribly lonesome and had no friends. The pastor listened patiently and finally, after hearing more of her life, said gently:

"Mary, I think I see why you are so lonesome. It is because you never wanted to be *bothered* with people. They are a bother because they do not agree with you that you are a poor social outcast. Your friends see you as an irritable, angry giant with whom very few people can safely associate without being swatted down!"

And with that, they both broke into laughter. Why? Because both took a quick look, not at a poor, little, unfortunate and broken child who had never been taught to relate to people, but at an egoist who was now embarrassed by her presumption and pride. The Biblically oriented perspective of the pastor was able to "spot" the problem. If the pastor had seen only her helplessness and responded to it with acceptance and understanding, she would have been left in her private hell of loneliness, except that the pastor would have jumped into it with her. Today, however, this woman is a radiant person who even describes herself as a "people-person." Before that could happen, she speaks of having "stopped fighting God for the number one spot in the world."

This woman discovered what the Bible is all about. The Bible sees man as rising up against God. Man is in rebellion, hoping to dethrone God and enthrone the human ego. Man has the freedom to rebel against God and such rebellion is sin. God's first word to man, therefore, is *repent,* for man is at war against God. God does not simply say *grow*, for the human predicament is not that man needs only to develop and evolve. He *is* evolved and full-grown as to his emotionality and humanity. Only the organically brain-damaged lack these gifts. We are not the ill-equipped, disadvantaged, embryonic people we think we are. Quite to the contrary, we have thought ourselves great enough to engage in a needless, foolish war with Ultimate Authority.

This is a crucial point, for what it means is that man's problem is not that he is misfunctioning because of his immaturity but that he is mispositioned in the world because of his arrogant pride. He is *over* God. My experience, personally and professionally, is that when one becomes correctly positioned *under* God, a person begins to straighten out inwardly (psychically) and outwardly (interpersonally). Egocentric pride, therefore, seems to be the root problem in human life.

There is no human way for us to free ourselves from our pride. The solution to the pride problem can only come by divine means working in a context of human despair. We shall have to look to the Highest Power and ask that His will be done and that His power (not our will power) save us. By means of this kind of surrender, we are brought for the first time to a subordinate position in the world. It is the position God intends for us.

If God is the answer, then I am not the answer. It is not my strength, my strategy, my knowledge, my skill that will save me and others. Nor will it help to use half human resource and half divine. We will have to abandon our egoistic machinations and rely only upon God, if we are to be saved.

It is for this reason that we say to a suffering person: One must die to prideful self in order to live again. I do not tell my parishioners to grow up. I do not say, "Live, in order to live;" I say, "Die, in order to live." To enjoin a person to grow whose basic problem is egocentricity is not only unhelpful but would seem to be immoral. Can we honestly believe we are helping a suffering person when we encourage and fortify his egoistic tendencies?

The dying to self must precede the new life under God. This is the way of the cross. The cross is the symbol of death. Our best known Christian symbol, the cross, was wisely chosen by the early Christians to convey the essence of the faith. Christians follow their Lord into the way of the cross (death) for "Do you not know that all of us who have been baptized into Christ Jesus were baptized into his death? We were buried therefore with him by baptism into death, so that as Christ was raised from the dead by the glory of the Father, we too might walk in newness of life" (Romans 6:3, 4).

The task of the counselor, therefore, would seem to be to offer the distressed individual ways to die to self. More specifically, it means to ask a person to consider what he wishes to surrender; what he wishes to let die; what sins he wishes to confess; what apologies he wishes to offer; what restitutions he wishes to make; when it is that he wishes to submit to terms other than his own. In a word, as a pastor, I set the stage for the death of a king. Until the king dies, he cannot live anew in the Kingdom whose King is God. If that sounds like a paraphrase of John 3:3 ("Unless one is born anew, he cannot see the kingdom of God"), it is supposed to!

Does all this exclude acceptance, love, understanding and trust in the helping relationship? Not at all. These are the very basis of our ministry to a person. Does this analysis wish to destroy identity? No, it is the paradoxical means unto it. Do I wish to destroy self-hate and help a person truly affirm his humanity by emerging from the chains of his inner bondage? I surely do. But the *way*, the method by which this is done is by the death of the prideful ego, the "phony me."

This is the strange paradox of the Gospel. We live by dying. We win by losing. We are saved by perishing. We triumph by surrendering. We come in first when we are last. God confounds all the calculations of human wisdom and knowledge. His ways are just the opposite of what we thought. They make us look foolish, "but God chose what is foolish in the world to shame the wise, God chose what is weak in the world to shame the strong, God chose what is low and despised in the world, even things that are not, to bring to nothing things that are, so that no human being might boast in the presence of God. He is the source of your life in Christ Jesus, whom God made our wisdom, our righteousness and sanctification and redemption; therefore, as it is written, 'Let him who boasts, boast of the Lord'" (I Corinthians 1:27-31).

11. The death of our freedom

We have already discussed the problem of human bondage—our inability to begin and cease at will. Paul said: "I can will what is right, but I cannot do it" (Romans 7:18). On the other hand, ". . . the evil I do not want is what I do" (verse 19). There is the problem. It is a problem of being in bondage to oneself, of not being free people—I mean people who want to begin something but are not free to carry out their plans; I mean people who desire to cease what they are doing and find it impossible to do so.

If we were free people, really free, our mental hospitals would be empty. There is not, to my knowledge, one emotional illness which could not be eradicated by inner freedom. The depressed person would be free from the tyranny of his gloomy thoughts. The drug addict would be free from his compulsion to take dope. The schizophrenic person would be free from that incessant bombardment of bizarre mental images. These people would be able to go and come at will, freely responding to their own desires.

I realize how grandiose these claims for inner, personal freedom sound. As a theory, it sounds too simplistic to deal with the myriad complexities of our human problems. But even if the theory looks good, is it not a rather absurd claim that we could bring people into such freedom? I would surely want to answer that question affirmatively because, obviously, no human help can ever really free us from our bondage.

But God can and does give us this freedom. The divine Christ claimed to reveal to us the way to true freedom. He began His ministry with the promise of our freedom. Listen to His grand claims:

"The Spirit of the Lord is upon me,
because he has anointed me to preach good news to the poor.
He has sent me to proclaim release to the captives
and recovering of sight to the blind,

101

to set at liberty those who are oppressed,
to proclaim the acceptable year of the Lord" (Luke 4:18, 19).
Later, he added,
". . . if the Son makes you free, you will be free indeed" (John 8:36)

Perhaps we are now ready to ask the question which comes from the deepest needs of our hearts.

How do we get this freedom?

And this is the answer: *We become free by letting our freedom die.*

Think about that.

We become free persons by giving up our freedom, by losing it. This is the paradox which is the stumbling block of most students of human behavior. Would not any rational man assert that to gain inner freedom, one must acquire more of it? Is it not reasonable and logical to take whatever freedom we possess and help it to grow and develop by every possible means? Human knowledge from the Greeks and Romans right down to present-day Freudianism has consistently encouraged us in this direction. Christ has not. He claimed a knowledge from above, a message from His Father, a word from another world—and it is quite contrary to our human expectation, for that paradoxical word sounds like this—

"So the last will be first, and the first last" (Matthew 20:16).

"For whoever would save his life will lose it, and whoever loses his life for my sake will find it" (Matthew 16:25).

". . . everyone who exalts himself will be humbled, but he who humbles himself will be exalted" (Luke 18:14).

"Truly, truly, I say to you, unless a grain of wheat falls into the earth and dies, it remains alone; but if it dies, it bears much fruit. He who loves his life loses it, and he who hates his life in this world will keep it for eternal life" (John 12:24, 25).

When we apply Christ's paradoxical way of thinking to the problem of freedom, we can only conclude that we receive true freedom by giving up our personal freedom to do as we wish and thereby submit to the "bondage" of terms other than our own. We become free by voluntarily giving up our freedom to live without authority (other than our own) over us. The ultimatized person (see diagram, page 29) aspires to be as free as God who is an authority to Himself. The price for this madness is bondage. Freedom from such bondage is given us when we cut a place in our lives for Authority and live our lives obediently under it. Let us now turn to a few examples to illustrate that freedom is given to those who lose it.

Tom was twenty pounds overweight. He had tried to control his weight for as long as he could remember, but with poor results. Lately, this problem had made him severely depressed. He wondered if somehow his self-control had completely left him.

A friend suggested to Tom that he go to his doctor and ask for help. At first this angered Tom but finally, after much procrastination he went to a physician who used a no-nonsense approach on him.

"Take these pills. Eat no more than 1200 calories a day. See me in three weeks."

"But doctor," protested Tom, "I think I need a gradual program!"

"Maybe you came to the wrong doctor, Tom. Is it your way or mine?"

(pause) "Yours, doctor," said Tom.

So Tom "lost" to the doctor. Tom gave up his freedom and voluntarily submitted to the control of the doctor. Tom normally gave himself the number one position in his world but now, because of his pain, he took the number two position and allowed the doctor to be his ultimate authority. The result was that for the first time, Tom was able to eat sensibly and lose weight. So Tom really won. Freedom comes by losing it.

A beautiful example of this is found in a lively letter published by *Faith at Work* Magazine (October-November, 1966). Mary Margaret Trevathan writes:

> I went to the Faith at Work conference at Gatlinburg and I have a new birthday, March 26. That was the night I gave up. Here were all these wonderful people, even my best friend from Columbia, South Carolina, who came to be with me, and I was miserable. I went back to my room, knelt by my bed and said, 'Okay, Lord, I give up; take over.' That night at the evening meeting the few words that I caught from Norman Grubb said to me that God's love can do anything and my part is to empty myself and let God's love work through me as His instrument.
>
> "It's wonderful! I'm free! I'm free to love people. They don't really have to love me back; it's nice when they do, but they don't have to because God loves me.
>
> I've lost ten pounds. My friends all know I've been trying to lose ten pounds for years and now those pounds are gone because I'm free of whatever it was that kept me snacking between, before, and after meals.
>
> I'm free of procrastination. This doesn't mean I'm caught up—I've been procrastinating for years. But I'm writing the

letters I used to put off. I have some straight drawers, and clean closets, and the kitchen and living room are usually presentable.

And the joy of it! To start every day with 'Good morning, Lord. What wonderful thing is going to happen today?' Some days it's a big thing, some days it's a small thing, but all days are good days.

I say with Paul, "Be like me." Free.[1]

Another interesting example which goes in the direction of freedom is illustrated by the work of Psychologist David F. Clark, as reported in *Time* Magazine, August 26, 1966, p. 46. The article is sufficiently brief to quote in its entirety.

Just about everyone swears on occasion. But some people are cursed with a pathological need to curse—and uncontrollably shout obscenities every few minutes. Accompanied by a violent muscular tic, their singular malady is called the Gilles de la Tourette syndrome for the French neurologist who first described it in 1884. The disease is rare, but its smutty symptoms turn its victims into social pariahs, and sometimes the psychological disorder leads them to mental institutions.

Investigators strongly suspect that the tic is neurotic in origin, related to the venting of aggression. Beginning in children as muscular twitches, the LaTourette syndrome gradually progresses to grunts and finally foul shouting. Doctors have tried everything from psychotherapy to sedatives and carbon dioxide inhalation, which is akin to a form of shock therapy. Lasting cures have proved as rare as the disease, but Psychologist David F. Clark now reports in the *British Journal of Psychiatry* that the treatment is contained in the symptoms.

Clark describes one patient, a man of 22, who could not control "his incessant and explosive repetition of our well-known monosyllabic obscenities loud enough to disturb others in rooms 30 yards away." Not surprisingly, the patient could not hold a job, appear in public or keep girl friends. Clark cured him by getting him to exaggerate his symptoms: He was made to repeat his favorite obscenities as loud and fast as he could until exhausted. Any alternative words or flagging from a metronome-paced cursing speed of up to 200 cusses a minute was discouraged by mild electric shocks.

The purpose of Clark's punishing therapy was to build up

---

[1] Used by permission of the author.

his patient's inhibition about his own symptoms: indeed the man has since passed a driving test without swearing at the woman examiner. Two of Clark's patients have not relapsed during four years since therapy, although neither had found relief during many previous years of psychotherapy. Clark's treatment only partly helped a third patient, a 47-year old housewife, because she was unwilling to swear on demand. Of course, restraining the symptoms may not be curing the disease; suppressed neuroses have a way of popping up in another form. But ulcers are certainly more socially acceptable than dirty words.[2]

From a pastoral point of view, the Gilles de la Tourette syndrome may be seen as a spiritual problem. There was a time in the history of the sufferer when he did not have the problem. As a human spirit possessing a freedom to choose, this person began to hear and then chose to use curse words. A whole set of contributory factors (environmental, psychic, emotional, hereditary) set the stage for the problem, but the person himself, out of his needs to enthrone his own ego, walked on the stage of his life and began to sing the song "Though It's Wrong, I Still Insist on Doing It." There was a sense of power that came from using profanity. It gave one a sense of being in control and this was worth the resulting sense of guilt. With continued profanity, came increasing bondage, for "every one who commits sin is a slave to sin" (John 8:34). Thereafter, cursing was compulsive.

The situation was altered by the appearance of an authority-person (the doctor) who offers the sufferer a choice between continuing under his own terms or submitting to the terms of an authority outside himself, namely, the doctor, and freely submitting to and acting upon his *absurd* suggestions. The doctor, by suggesting an intense program of cursing, contradicts the sufferer's incessant struggle to cease cursing. The doctor counsels the sufferer to *increase* the cursing and that, indeed, he will be punished if he fails to curse less than 200 times a minute! Notice that the fourty-seven-year-old housewife who "was unwilling to swear on demand," was only partly helped. Others, who were willing, were much helped. I suggest that the reason for this is that certain sufferers had the faith to give up their freedom, the reward for which is that they became free of their symptoms.

What took place in Dr. Clark's "successes," however, would seem to be an amelioration of the problem rather than a cure, as *Time* suggests. The symptoms were restrained but a cure was not

---

[2] *Time* Magazine, August 26, 1966 issue.

effected. I think this is quite generally characteristic of the medical approach to emotional illness. Psychiatry and psychology do effect an ameliorative change in people, but it would seem that the reason for such changes can be explained by the authority-role of the healer rather than his knowledge and expertise. Apparently, the major benefits received from the professional are due only incidentally to his skill. We know, for example, that even when we withhold psychiatric treatment from people in mental hospitals, giving them merely custodial care, 70 per cent will improve enough to be on their way again.[3] We also know that emotionally ill people will receive a tangible and sometimes dramatic relief from their symptoms just by submitting to psychotherapy, regardless of the training, personality or orientation of the psychotherapist. The various schools of psychotherapy all claim about the same rate of success, though they differ widely in approach. What this means, it seems to me, is that just by coming to terms in some way with an authority-structure, people receive a degree of help. That help will not penetrate to the heart of the illness until the god-problem is addressed, but yet it is in the right direction.

Before a final illustration of positioning-under-authority is given, I would like to stress two points—one concerning the suffering person and the other concerning the use of authority by the helping person.

The suffering person, before he can really be helped, must come to an acceptance of his problem. He must admit that there is a problem and that he has it. This is extremely difficult for all of us and we have all kinds of ways of hedging and even denying what we really have. Instead of a flat statement like "I am a homosexual," a person will say, "I *think* I am a homosexual" or "I am a little bit homosexual." Such tactics are similar to the young, maiden lady who told her doctor that she thought she was "just a little bit pregnant." When the doctor finally talked her out of that one, she insisted that this must be one of those very rare cases of virgin birth!

The truth about ourselves is very painful to accept. It is excruciatingly painful to our egos to make statements like "I am overweight," "I am a liar," "I am an adulterer." Until we, by the grace of God, finally reach a point where we can say "I have this problem," we are beyond the reach of those who would help us.

---

[3] Jerome Frank, *Persuasion and Healing,* Baltimore: Johns Hopkins Press, 1961, p. 14. Cf. also pp. 35 ff. for a description of how alcoholics who voluntarily admit themselves to a hospital, lose their compulsion to drink within about ten days, even before an active treatment program has begun.

Whatever they say to us passes by us because it is intended for the people who *are* something, while *we* are not yet in that category, we keep assuring ourselves.

If that kind of truthfulness is expected of the sufferer, we must also expect some basic truthfulness in the helping person concerning his person and role. I will not elaborate on the fact that the helper must have the same kind of self-honesty about what he *has,* as the one being helped. He should also have found real solutions to whatever problems he *has.* But there is added to this, an additional kind of honesty necessary concerning the authority-role of the helper.

A helper in the healing arts (pastor, doctor, AA sponsor, counselor) should clearly understand that he only represents authority. He is not authority. Only God is authority. Certain people may be appointed by their fellows to represent authority to them, but that authority never finds its source in the appointee. The professional healer is a servant, carrying divine authority to needy people. The professional does this *only by being in his role*, and so, to the degree that the sufferer submits to the authority vested by God in any professional, there will be some ameliorative healing.

Sadly, however, help from the professional becomes contaminated and eventually nullified if he does not recognize himself as an agent, and *only* an agent, of God's power and authority. What happens in the case of the self-enthroned professional is that he (1) makes an assumption that he is omnicompetent; (2) attempts to heal out of the resources of his own skill, power and authority; (3) teaches the sufferer to imitate his own egocentric style of life. The result is that what benefit was received by capitulation to the authority vested in the professional is nullified by the professional's egoistic attempts to play god. The only reason God vests authority in us is so that we might lead people back to Him. Any authority-person in the healing arts, therefore, who has it as his purpose to bring real freedom to suffering people, will need to bring people to himself only to quickly lead them to God who can make them free.

And now, a final illustration demonstrating the principle of freedom through "bondage."

This is the case of Bob, a man who could not stop hating his father. He was hooked on hate. I listened by the hour to this man while he poured out his resentment and bitterness toward his father. At the point where we will pick up the recorded conversation, Bob is complaining that his father did not send him to a school for airplane mechanics.

BOB: After two years at sea, I came home. I asked him to send me to school. He told me to go work my way through.

I: Your father wanted you to stand on your own two feet.

BOB: But I help *my* sons through school. Why didn't he?

I: He is a different generation.

BOB: No, I resent my Dad.

I: Bob, you have made your point. Now I have a suggestion. It is this—that you consider going to your father and asking his pardon for all the tons of hate and criticism you have heaped upon him all these years. He never deserved it. Consider asking his forgiveness for your ingratitude.

BOB: (a long silence) Maybe I had better do it. I will.

It was apparent to me that God was working in Bob for he was losing to me—to me as a representative of God. The next step was to invite Bob to lose directly to God and that went like this:

BOB: I joined the Episcopal Church but it never felt right. I drifted away.

I: Yes. Your life has been one long argument with God in which you have insisted on going your own way. You were in competition with God.

BOB: That's a serious sin. Maybe I should confess it. I once read about confession in the prayer book. I think I need it.

I: I agree with you. At your signal we can begin.

BOB: It will take hours.

I: I have the time.

BOB: I want to.

I: Let us begin.

In this example of precounseling with Bob, the thing to note is that by playing the part of authority-surrogate and by means of my suggestion that Bob apologize to his father, becoming reconciled to him, I presented terms to him other than his own. I gave Bob something and someone with whom he could come to terms. Admittedly, this is to bring him to a point of capitulation, but this is not at all to humiliate or destroy him—rather, it is *the* opportunity for him to freely "lose" and thereby truly win. Today Bob is a free man—free from hate, from alcohol and free to act humanly. His confession was spoken with tears and agonizing pain. Bob has thrown over the controls of his life to God. In losing control to God we find true personal freedom. If we are under Control, we function well. If we are our own control, we are in bondage to ourselves.

12. The death of our egoism

Heaven knows I tried everything. But I've come to one conclusion. I don't need any more religion—nor any more psychiatry. I've had about all I can take from psychiatrists and also pastors like you, Chaplain.

What I need now is God. Just God.

A patient in a mental hospital

We have been talking about surrender. There are dangers in such an act.

One danger is that the surrender is made under the guidance of a person who himself is unsurrendered to God. If the one through whom the surrender is made is himself a self-enthroned egoist, he will then counsel the surrendered person to imitate his life-style. Jesus spoke about casting out one devil, only to have seven rush in after the house is clean. ". . . the last state of that man becomes worse than the first . . ." (Matthew 12:45).

Another danger is that the surrender be made to another human being, with God out of the picture altogether. This would quickly bring us back into bondage. Our surrender should always be *unto* God. Perhaps we should speak of surrender or submission unto the Lord *through* people, which is plainly the thought of Christ's teaching. That people should vicariously represent God was in the mind of Christ when he said: " 'Truly, I say to you, as you did it to one of the least of these my brethren, you did it to me' " (Matthew 25:40).

If surrender is made *to* God *through* the instrumentality of a Christian, that Christian being himself a dethroned egoist, then the one surrendering will be brought to God in order to repent and freely confess his sin. Repentance and confession unto God must be added to surrender. Surrender to God means only that the sinner has ceased his war with God and that the sinner now stands ready to accept God's terms. What remains is for our egoism to be crucified with Christ and this comes about through repentance and confession. Presently, however, we are considering that act of surrender. We can observe the act of capitulation in the following recording of an alcoholic in a group encounter.

HE: I've made up my mind to leave this hospital. I refuse to stay the six weeks. Two is enough. I've even prayed about this matter, and I feel it is God's will that I leave.

GROUP MEMBER: Did you get a message from Him?

HE: This is beyond your and my understanding. I've been praying a long time.

GROUP MEMBER: You felt something.

HE: No, I just believe I should leave.

I: Well, I must be on the side of the devil because I applied for and received permission for you to stay six weeks. We won't hold you in chains, however, if you wish to leave. But the way is open to stay.

GROUP MEMBER: You once told the pastor you would stay six weeks.

I: This is the story of his life—house, money, boat, alcohol—everything before his own soul. Your life is at stake again. Look, if you go out of here, you don't stand a ghost of a chance. I will feel guilty if I turn you loose!

HE: What makes you think four more weeks here will help? What miracle are you going to perform?

I: I perform no miracles. But I know this—you have not begun to deal with your pride.

HE: I don't have any pride left.

GROUP MEMBER: Isn't it funny how we resent most what is true—what we fear most. What sort of miracle do you expect if you leave early?

HE: I don't expect one. What guarantee do I have that if I stay I will not fall flat on my face again?

I: All we can do is work and pray. Work and pray.

Immediately after this encounter, our friend was so shaken up that he asked for a private conference. We met the next day in my study and it soon became evident that he was learning the beginning of true humility.

HE: I have decided to stay six weeks. At our last meeting I got pretty angry. What is the matter with me? What is my basic trouble? I am all confused, to tell the truth.

I: That is a straight question—I'll try to give you a straight answer. You are in a delusion about yourself. You diminish the size of your staggering problems and magnify your capacity to deal with them. You are in a fantasy—that is why you fall on your face.

HE: I have proved that. I feel so ashamed of myself. Last year particularly I hurt so many people. If I could only go back.
I: No man can.
HE: I would give my right arm to stop drinking. I need plain guts.
I: I disagree. You tried guts. Guts will not do it. This is so big a problem that we will have to place it in the hands of God Almighty. You and your guts are no match.
HE: I guess you are right. (silence) Tell me what to do.

This man had reached a point of capitulation, of surrender. He was brought to that point wholly by God. I just stood there, trying to be honest and open, restraining myself from any use of manipulative counseling techniques. God did the work of humbling this man to a point where he became *teachable*. "Tell me what to do."

"I suggest," I said softly, "a full confession to God, spoken in my presence."

"But Reverend! I'm a Protestant, not a Roman Catholic," he protested. "Why can't I just confess to God in my prayers? I was taught that confession is to God. It isn't necessary to confess to anyone else to receive forgiveness if I am truly sorry."

You notice that the war is not yet over, not by any means! This is because the surrender always comes by degrees. There is an astonishing amount of rebellion left in even the most surrendered of us. My suggestion, a tough one, transported us both to a new battle ground on which a decision would have to again be made either to make war or surrender.

Why did I make this bold suggestion to this suffering alcoholic? Because it is a door through which all alcoholics must enter, according to Alcoholics Anonymous, if they wish to live again. The most difficult of the Twelve Steps is the fifth: "Admitted to God, to ourselves and to another human being the exact nature of our wrongs."

Let us clearly understand that just as surrender is always to God, so is auricular (spoken into the ear of another) confession always to God. The person into whose ear the confession is spoken is simply a *witness* of the the confession which the penitent person is making to God. I do not know of a single AA sponsor, nor any pastor who would be so arrogant as to say that confessions are made to him and that he has the power to pardon as a function of his person. Only God can pardon sin. We people who minister to others and who ourselves are in need of forgiveness, can but testify to what God alone can do.

It would be helpful at this point to list a few of the benefits of auricular confession.

1. *Auricular confession destroys pride as nothing else will.* We all understand how difficult it is to confess to God silently. If silent prayer is sincere, it will reduce our pride somewhat. There is, however, a more difficult way of confession—one which will not merely reduce pride but destroy it. It is done by speaking openly of our sins in the hearing of another sinner. I can assure you that something dies in us when we do this! It is the old man in us, the proud self. His death is excruciatingly painful and often violent. Honest moral inventory of this kind shakes us up, even causes us to despair, but never breaks us or demolishes us, for God makes us to live again by His power, even as we die.

When, by God's grace, my parishioner chooses this difficult but necessary death, I know that he is truly humble. He is empty of self. The grandiose delusions, the lies, the phoniness, the pride—they no longer work. Neither is there need for them. The confessing person is now true, humble, honest.

Confession empties us of pride as nothing else will. Humility, which is the opposite of pride, is not something we can talk ourselves into—it is the result of deeds. When our Lord wished to teach His disciples about humility, He did not preach a sermon; rather, He acted it out by the deed of washing their feet. Even He humbled Himself. Must we always be humbled by the chastening of the Lord through the violent crises of life or might we elect to be humbled through the deed of making an auricular confession?

2. *Auricular confession stops the flow of easy, empty words.* I estimate that in an hour of counseling, a parishioner and I will exchange about 4,500 words. Some of these words are necessary and carry much meaning but, frankly, many of them are superfluous. It is always so in human dialogue. We usually use words extravagantly, not to mention recklessly and at times, deceptively, for we frequently use words to construct a "front" to properly impress the people with whom we deal. My parishioner and I use a good amount of our words to "present" ourselves to each other.

All this stops when the confessing person is turned away from the eyes of his human witness and addresses God directly. I give recognition to the dialogue with God (as I will explain in the following chapter) by turning away from the eyes of my parishioner. He is no longer speaking to me. I am only a human witness. Now all the easy talk ceases. Each word must be mined from the depths of his soul. It makes no sense to create a "front" or to impress or manipulate me for I am out of the picture and to try these tactics on God is invariably understood as making a fool of one's self. Now each word carries its full depth of meaning and the cost for this man, at times, is heartrending and agonizing.

3. *Auricular confession confirms that one has been honest with God.*

It is very difficult for us to realize and accept the fact that we have a terrible time being honest with ourselves and with God. We need a confidant who is willing to help us with our evasions, equivocations and rationalizations when we confess to the Judge of all the earth. Our temptation is to bend the truth and evade reality. Another person, even though he may not say a word, is a reminder to be honest with God. This is why it is far easier to confess privately to God than in another person's presence. That "other human person" keeps one honest.

In my own experience, I recall once deliberately lying to my confessor because a certain issue was too painful to put into words. I have never felt like such a fool in my entire life! To actually *hear* the spoken lie, smote me. If I had not spoken my lie into the ear of my confessor, I am quite sure my deception with God would have "succeeded."

4. *Auricular confession brings one back into the human community.*

"In confession the break-through to community takes place. Sin demands to have a man by himself. It withdraws him from the community. The more isolated a person is, the more destructive will be the power of sin over him, and the more deeply he becomes involved in it, the more disastrous is his isolation. Sin wants to remain unknown. It shuns the light. In the darkness of the unexpressed it poisons the whole being of a person."[1]

Sin against one member of the human community and you are estranged from all its members. Confess in the presence of one and you are united to all. That seems to be a law which God has placed in the world.

5. *Auricular confession gives us the benefit of the witness' counsel.* After a full confession, we shall need advice and counsel. "Only by being willing to take advice and accept direction can we set foot on the road to straight thinking, solid honesty and genuine humility."[2]

[1] Dietrich Bonhoeffer, *Life Together,* New York: Harper and Row, 1954, p. 112.

[2] Alcoholics Anonymous Fellowship, *Twelve Steps and Twelve Traditions,* Alcoholics Anonymous Inc., 1953, p. 60.

6. *Auricular confession assists us in feeling forgiven.*

Few people know this feeling. All desire it.

People who have it possess abiding peace of soul. When the sense of pardon penetrates deeply into a person, God means everything to him. All men may experience this but only a small remnant of humanity come to know it.

Robert Raines tells us how he came to an assurance of pardon. "During the course of a conversation, I told my friend about my lack of assurance and asked if he would serve as my confessor. He agreed to do so. I told him in detail the matter of concern. He listened, questioned me, and then prayed for me. It was a prayer of absolution, a declaration of forgiveness, the visible and audible assurance, in a brother who forgives, of the Lord who forgives. This was a liberating experience for me and in the days that followed, the assurance of forgiveness *did* come."[3]

A great man of God, Samuel M. Shoemaker, said the following in a sermon shortly before the end of his long and fruitful ministry: ". . . the thing to do with sin is to do what Nicodemus did: go and search out someone with whom we can talk privately and frankly. Tell them of these things and, with them, to God. You say that you can do this alone with God; and I ask you, Have you succeeded in doing so? I said I was going to do that for years, but it never happened until I let a human witness come in on my decision. That is the 'how' of getting rid of sin if you are in earnest about doing it at all; face it, share it, surrender it, hate it, forsake it, confess it, and restore for it."[4]

Quite understandably, we object to the third party—a human ear who hears the confession. Why is that human ear so necessary? I'll never forget how one recovered alcoholic answered that question. This man, whose years of alcoholism plainly showed on his face, gave the best answer I have ever heard.

"Well, it's this way—God already knows what you've done so there is no sense to telling just Him. What you have to do is tell your sins to someone who doesn't know them yet."

That says it.

---

[3] Robert Raines, *Reshaping the Christian Life,* New York: Harper and Row, 1964, p. 133.

[4] Charles L. Wallis, Editor, *Eighty-Eight Evangelistic Sermons,* New York: Harper and Row, 1964, p. 82.

13. The death of our guilt

"Pastor, before I go, may I make a full confession? I feel I will burst if I don't."

Another person said: "I am in despair over what I have done. What should I do now, Pastor?"

The first question was asked by a woman about a week ago. A man asked the second question last year. Both of these people were in my study, though at different times. With a gesture of my hand, I pointed to a small table against the wall. This table is the size of a small desk and is covered with a white linen. The Bible lies open on it and behind it is a bronze cross. On either side of the cross are two candles.[1]

I invite those who wish to confess to God in my presence to sit before this table. One doing this faces a visual field which is restricted to Christian symbols on the table. The whole idea of the confessional is that one turns away from man and addresses God. For this reason, I am seated behind the parishioner and slightly to the right. By this arrangement we are both reminded that the dialogue is with God, while I as a pastor am only a confidential witness. It is necessary, however, to first give the parishioner an explanation of how to proceed.

When the person is seated before the table and I am out of the line of vision, I say something like this:

"You and I are in the presence of God. Let your body relax completely for a few minutes and open your spirit to experience God's presence. (pause) What we talk about here will always be a secret with us. I assure you that you are completely safe in my presence to reveal anything to God. (pause) I encourage you to speak of anything which has been hidden; anything for which you feel regret; anything for which you feel guilty. This is a time to be completely open with God. (pause) You may begin when you

---

[1] See the diagram on the following page.

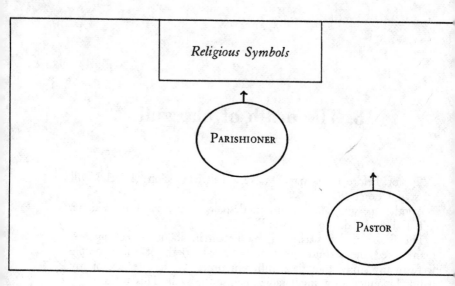

The Confessional Arrangement—Diagram No

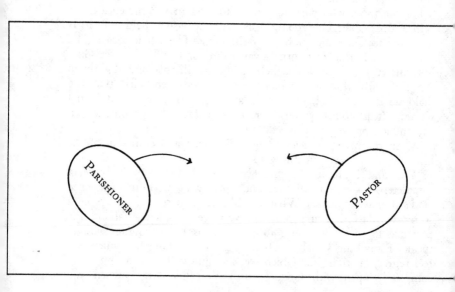

The Counseling Arrangement—Diagram No

wish—or, wait for a time. We have plenty of time. There is no hurry. When you finish speaking, indicate to me that you are finished.

Then I am silent and while we are waiting, I pray for this person who, by the mercy of God, is now displaying such mangificent courage—a courage combined with an exquisite humility.

And then, slowly, each burdened word is lifted to God.

No pastor would ever divulge what he hears, but I can say this—the depth of revelation is far greater in the confessional than I have ever experienced in face to face counseling. When one realizes that he is in dialogue with God, a new seriousness comes into the parisioner's verbal communication; he economizes on easy words in this situation. He meets God in the realization that it is utter folly and worse, a foul trick on himself, to evade or distort the truth about himself. The confessional provides the opportunity to go to the depths, and my experience has been that people really do just that, provided their pride has been sufficiently discarded.

I sit in silence until my brother or sister has finished speaking the heretofore unspeakable. Sometimes one finishes in minutes but another may speak for an hour before he indicates that he is finished.

Let us try to understand how one feels when the confession is finished. The most common feeling is the fear of over-revelation—that one has spoken too much and is now dangerously exposed. It is also the feeling of having thrown one's life on the table and wondering now what to do with it. Frightening questions may arise in this person's heart—"Now that all this is on the table, how will I ever get it off again? *Can* it be removed?"

At such a point I begin to speak, for it is now my privilege to communicate to this choice person the Gospel of Jesus Christ with its strong, comforting assurances of pardon. Up to this point in the confessional, I have been an ear hearing a soul speak to God but now I become a voice witnessing to the forgiveness of God in Christ. That is all I am—a voice. Not the source of forgiveness, not the dispenser of grace, not the absolver of sins—just a voice speaking somewhat as follows:

"I am a witness to your confession to God. God has promised forgiveness and pardon to those who sincerely confess their sins, as I believe you have. The Holy Scriptures tell us: 'If we confess our sins, [God] is faithful and just, and will forgive our sins and cleanse us from all unrighteouness'" (I John 1:9).

"Do you believe this with all your heart?" I pause for his answer. If there is doubt, we immediately discuss it. But if his answer is affirmative, then I continue:

"Now place your hand on the Scriptures before you as a sign that you believe the promises of God. With your other hand, hold tightly the cross before you as a sign of your faith in our Lord Jesus Christ."

"Let us now pray for grace and offer thanksgiving. Please repeat after me."

"Lord Jesus Christ: Thou hast heard me speak of my sins. I ask Thee to pardon them completely, through Thy blood shed on the cross. Remove every spot of guilt and save my soul by Thy perfect atonement. I thank Thee for this salvation. Thou art now my Leader and my God. I am Thy follower. I surrender to Thee. In the Name of the Father, and of the Son, and of the Holy Spirit. Amen."

I continue with these quiet words: "I want you always to remember this day—and how your hand is on the cross and on the Bible. This is the day of a new beginning, of a new life. Your sins are forgiven. That chapter of your life is now finished. It is a closed book. Now you may begin to live."

The confession is finished, but now the pastoral counsel begins. I ask my parishioner to turn around so that we may talk face to face. (See Diagram #2) We have much about which to talk. A person does not go through such an experience without gathering many reactions.

One of the reactions may be a lingering sense of guilt for the things confessed. Such a person may return to speak again and again of the guilt-producing act or feeling. Sometimes it is enough for the pastor simply to say: "It is *finished* now. It is finished business. Let it die. Close that chapter of your life."

This will not always suffice, however, and so it may be that there are obstacles of deeper sin, and particularly, of deeper pride, which may be causing the conflict. Indeed, this conflict may be unconscious to the parishioner and we may have to return time after time to the confessional, perhaps on a weekly basis. Slowly, however, the unconscious becomes conscious. We may rest assured that this exercise in honesty will in no way harm a person psychically, nor will this push him into a psychosis. This kind of damage happens when people are forced in some way to say what they are not ready to say or have someone disclose to them something they are not ready to see. All this is foreign to the complete permissiveness which the confessional offers. We may be sure, therefore, that *whatever* a person is able to freely speak about in the confessional, he is ready to himself hear, and that without any danger to his mind or emotions.

As I witness a person confessing to God, I make mental notes of ways in which this person can be helped. A knowledge of the

Bible, an understanding of people, good theological training, a disciplined spiritual life, sanctified common sense—these are now indispensable, but not always in my possession. But this I do know—that this is not a time for lengthy explanations. There is no need to explain what makes people tick. It is of little profit to tell a person the early origins of his conflicts for this is now an academic issue. There is no point explaining defense mechanisms and this person's interpersonal strategems, nor the games he and other people play. Let us understand that God has just released this person from the prison of his guilt and now he is *free*. A wise pastor, it seems to me, will concentrate on ways in which this new person in Christ can use his freedom.

In order to help the confessing person make a concrete use of his freedom, the pastor should be prepared to make certain appropriate suggestions to the parishioner. These suggestions should grow out of the content of the confession. Surely a number of things mentioned call for some action and it seems to me a crucial point that the pastor suggest certain actions rather than that the parishioner outline his own program of action. The reason for this is simply that the parishioner needs something from without himself to which he can submit. If no such suggestions are made from without, the parishioner has no recourse but to act out of his own authority and according to his own plans, thereby depriving himself of the freedom which the loss of his freedom grants.

What is the nature of these pastoral suggestions? Most frequently, they are suggestions to make restitution to people whom the parishioner has wronged. If, for example, money has been stolen, the suggestion would be to begin repaying it, even if in very small amounts. Or perhaps the parishioner confessed the sin of character assasination. He should be encouraged to make apology and make an effort to reestablish the offended one's good name. I frequently suggest, in cases where people have wronged their parents, to go to them and become reconciled. Almost invariably, I suggest that the parishioner soon meet with me again and though this is admittedly a low-order suggestion, it nonetheless provides the new man an opportunity to respond to a suggestion from outside himself and submit to an authority other than his own. In this almost primitive way, we help a person to concretely submit to God as He is represented through the role of the pastor.

The suggestions of the pastor to the parishioner should always be considerate—considerate of the abilities and the situation of the parishioner. Great care should be taken never to suggest the impossible and surely never the absurd or frivolous. The restitution, reconciliation, apology or whatever it is that is suggested should always be within range. The pastor ought to be aware of the effect which his acted-on suggestion might have on others. If others are harmed by the pastoral counsel, better it were not offered in the first place. There is wisdom in the Ninth Step of the AA program: "Made direct amends to such people [whom we have harmed] except when to do so would injure them or others."

We are assuming, therefore, that the pastor is a wise and compassionate man in offering post-confessional counsel. Is not this a gratuitous assumption and is it not contradicted by the bungling of quite a few? I am sure it would be true in the case of pastors who themselves are mispositioned, having never experienced the dying brought about by confession. And therefore it must be something of a rule, it seems to me, that no man should undertake to hear confessions unless he himself regularly submits himself to this spiritual discipline. What is more incongruous and disastrous than to have an enthroned egoist witness and then react to the destruction of egoism in another person? The danger of this happening is reduced only to the degree that the pastor is himself correctly positioned under God and with people. Given a pastor who is solidly positioned under the Lordship of Christ; given a pastor who has died as to his own freedom, egoism and guilt; given a pastor who continues to do such dying—then there is little danger that the counsel offered will do any damage. Indeed, it will do the parishioner eternal good.

Returning for a moment to this matter of making amends and restitution for past wrongs, the parishioner who listens to his own counsel in these matters often runs into trouble. Usually, without realizing it, the parishioner becomes punitive toward himself, suggesting and sometimes pleading to do things which are at best inappropriate, and at their worst, cruel. Cruel, that is, to himself, not to mention others. This kind of severity is not an evidence of piety or true contrition. It is that old devil *self-atonement* intruding himself even into this sacred moment when the miracle of conversion is taking place. It is the pastor's task, therefore, to suggest appropriate action—things to do within the range of the new man in Christ.

Contemplate that new man in Christ. Confession has left his heart clean, fresh and at peace. The anxiety caused by guilt is quieted. The conscience no longer accuses. Delusional pride and arrogance have been dealt a mortal blow. The confessing believer knows the peace which passes understanding.

There are also a few gleanings from the rich harvest for the pastor. His calling is confirmed. Simultaneously, he feels dignity and humility. There is no more confusion now about what a pastor *does*—a pastor walks the *via dolorosa* with his people to the cross where the perfect atonement was made by the Lamb of God that taketh away the sin of the world. After that, the pastor sits as a spectator as God raises up one dead man after another.

14. The death of loneliness

There is another death of which we must speak: the death of our loneliness. The self-enthroned egoist is the loneliest person in the world. He suffers poignantly and incessantly with deep spiritual pain. This is the pain of which the existentialists speak as they describe how it feels to exist all alone in a dark, meaningless world in which all hope of real personal relationships with God and fellow man are gone. David Riesman speaks of our plight as he describes the lonely crowd. Most sensitive spirits sense that we all have become islands. This is our tragedy—that we do not really know each other.

Small wonder.

We sent God into exile. We then made our fellows either opponents or stepping stones. In the case of the first, we knocked people down; in the second instance, we built people up; but in either case, it was always with our self-elevation in mind. Inevitably the consequence, however, was loneliness.

I believe that God established His church in this world to bring about an end to our loneliness. The church is a *community* in which God dwells with His people. Our loneliness and isolation was the need which occasioned the church. God does not need a church. *We* do. God foresaw our need and prepared the church from the foundations of the world as the instrument through which we would live in fellowship and unity, to the praise of His Name.

Let us attempt to describe God's church in its most essential form. This is difficult to do in a day when "church" means anything from a building to a complex denominational structure to a group of people worshiping together on a Sunday morning. None of these ideas, it seems to me, really describes the essential church—that instrument through which our loneliness will die.

What does a church resemble in its simplest, yet complete form? A church is a small group of people, ideally five to eight in number, who interact with each other under the guidance of the Holy Spirit.

The interaction is usually by means of verbal communication, a communication which is characterized by openness, honesty and trust. Words, however, must eventually issue in deeds done to and for themselves and others.

The church is a *working* group whose purpose is spiritual growth to the glory of God.

Each member aims at self-disclosure, for this is the only way to know and be known. To one person, this means a confession of sin. Another shares a problem in living, *his* problem—not others. Someone else will want to share feelings of joy over some gift from the Lord. Another person will express his discontentedness and resentment. The listening members will want to respond with honest reactions, parallel experiences, suggestions and advice either to encourage or discourage a course of action, for everyone feels he is his brother's keeper.

A church is a trustworthy guardian of shared confidences.

The church is a fellowshiping, joy-generating assembly of people who hold Jesus Christ as their common Lord. Through Him they are a forgiven and forgiving community.

God's church is a spiritual family. We live together intimately. We talk to each other in such a way that human spirit touches human spirit.

When the church is assembled, human spirits join in fellowship and conversation (prayer) with the Divine Spirit. God hears and answers those prayers.

And finally, consider that a church is nothing without God. That is to say, God is always being dealt with by the members of the church. Perhaps I can best explain this by relating a recent experience of my wife in a small group. A middle-aged man presented in detail a sizeable problem in his business life. The group leader responded with this question: "Have you prayed about this problem?" This very ordinary question struck my wife, Joan, as such an appropriate and helpful question to ask the man. She went on to say that there was a time when she would almost scream when that kind of question was asked. It had sounded so inane, so "religious." But now, in this gathering, in this church, it made all kinds of sense. This was the leader's effort to help the businessman deal with God. Without God, the church could not function. Without God, the problem could not be solved. God was understood as the center of the life of the church.

A group can gather, you understand, and not deal with God. God is then left out, ignored. I have both participated in and observed many such groups enough times to know the difference between a church and a group of talking individuals who are a self-contained unit with no conscious recognition of or appeal to God.

For a period of four years I was a member of a psychoanalytically oriented psychotherapy group which was led by an analyst whose philosophic outlook was humanistic. Quite understandably, he was interested only in the interpersonal processes and healthy psychic functioning. At that period of my life, I was fascinated with people and what made them tick. The study of man intrigued me and no small part of my interest was the gifted, versatile mind of the therapist to whom I willingly paid my money so that I could observe him and learn his secrets.

This particular therapist had one of the sharpest intellects I have ever known. His explanations of our interpersonal behavior was sometimes brilliant, always clever. He dazzled all of us—or was it that we were enchanted by him? Anyway, we gladly followed him as he searched out the roots of our neuroses. With him, we asked a simple question of ourselves—"Why?" We never answered it but we liked the question and the possibility of an answer to it. Our therapist would treat a sick member of the group by asking probing questions. Soon we were all treating people in the group whom we thought were sick. We called this "empathy" and "understanding" and "helping a person face reality." We were, myself included, enthusiastic devotees of a humanistic psychology which ignored Deity as a significant reality in the world.

I am now very sure that what I experienced in this group was surely not psychotherapy at its best. I know religiously oriented psychotherapists who work quite differently and really help their patients on a deep level. A therapist who makes a place for God in his own life and teaches his patients to do the same, is quite different from my experience with this group whose ultimate devotion was to Man and to this therapist who functioned as a high priest of humanism.

As I look back on my experience with humanistic psychotherapy, I have two particular reactions. The first is that so much of what we did in group therapy was mainly a brain-game. Now, maybe that was my fault and my problem. Some have claimed deep emotional insight and healing from the group in which I was a member. Indeed, I also felt so at the time and there was no question about it—it was better than what I had. It was a more self-aware and sophisticated brand of humanism than I had concocted through the years! But those were the days when I still had not enthroned God as the Lord of my life.

A second reaction is that this kind of psychotherapy can only go so far. Its limits are man and his knowledge of himself. Now there are some things in this for which we can be grateful, I am sure, but the great danger of which most people are quite unaware is that such an approach tends to ultimatize man in the world. When God is not recognized as a *working* God and the *only* ultimate help for our problematic lives, then *we* will work and *we* will solve our problems and *we* will overcome—but not really.

In my own life, it became clear to me that my "work" was not doing the job. I have also come to realize that the really big problems of my life are *beyond* my solution. It has also gotten through to me that God will have to save and heal me if my salvation for this world and the next is to be accomplished. I cannot *do* anything, other than surrender myself to God, to save myself. If I *do* something, I will perish. Difficult as it is to restrain my deep desire to be activistic, I now realize that only by *not* doing what seems so apparently needful, will I be saved.

The small-group church of which I am speaking keeps reminding me of these tested truths. The people in it support and counsel me as I "wait for the Lord." This church, of which I speak, knows its task. How God uses it to bring about the death of our isolation and loneliness! Let me tell you about the particular church to which I belong.

It has no name, nor denominational affiliation.

It is small—five married couples.

We meet once a week for an hour and fifteen minutes. Membership lasts only for six weeks. After that, one may again join the fellowship if he promises to attend all the meetings.

We talk—but only about matters of genuine concern to each individual. One has a problem in his work. Another is frustrated. Still another has a deep martial conflict or, perhaps, a sexual problem. Raising children may be another's problem. The whole range of human problems is fit material for our meeting, but in general we try to concentrate on the areas in our lives which give us pain. In fact, we usually delay dealing with the really painful life-problems until our time of meeting, because we all understand that there is less danger of a needless explosion in church. I cannot imagine any problem too great or too dangerous for this church to handle. It is, moreover, a praying church. Indeed, prayer is the most important thing we do.

A striking feature of this church is that it is not led by a human person. To be sure, one of us functions as an administrative leader. The time of meetings must be set. All meetings must terminate at a set time unless a group decision is made to continue.

The "leader" arranges these housekeeping details. This is what is meant by an administrative leader. In no sense, however, is he a therapist-type leader. In fact, though some of us are pastors, none of us function as such. The real leadership of this church is in the hands of the Holy Spirit. He leads us, through the gathering of assembled Christians, meeting in His name. "For where two or three are gathered in my name, there am I in the midst of them" (Matthew 18:20).

Such a *koinonia* (close fellowship group) is the best kind of pastor for the flock of Christ. If my understanding of the church is correct, the small group can not only perform almost every function of an individual pastor, but even more, the small group can do pastoral work more effectively than a single pastor.

Consider, to cite some support for this position, that the wisdom of a *koinonia* group is superior to the wisdom of one pastor. One individual, though he be trained and ordained, is always subject to a kind of bias and delusional distortion from which the group is usually much more free. In the matter of understanding and teaching the word of God, a gathering of Christians can do this themselves far better than a sermon by a pastor. Or again, if we agree that the major tasks of the Christian pastor are sustaining, healing and shepherding, then I would like to argue that a small group of Christians can do this work better for themselves than an individual pastor. Even in such a matter as declaring a person's sins forgiven, this can be done by any committed Christian. Dr. Paul Tournier, a Christian psychiatrist, is correct, it seems to me, in declaring absolution in the name of God to a patient who has made a confession of sin in his presence.[1]

Then, too, when one thinks of the need for keeping confidence, I have found small groups of Christians to be eminently confidential. A person needing a confidential situation may find it easier to speak to one person rather than a small group, but this is because of spiritual weakness and timidity rather than the incompetence of the group to grant him confidentiality. And finally, consider how individual pastors come and go, but a small group is a continuing organism which continues to function and grow under the Holy Spirit no matter which member leaves.

What, then, is the purpose of having an ordained pastor in a church? I can think of at least two reasons, both of them rather humbling to the professional dignity we attach to being a clergyman. The first justification for a pastor, aside from the scriptural

---

[1] Paul Tournier, *Guilt and Grace,* New York: Harper and Row, 1962, p. 205.

mandate concerning his office, is that the gathered church needs a servant—one who can minister, one who arranges things for others. As a pastor, he is called upon to set the stage for great spiritual dramas to take place. God and His people are the actors. Now the pastor is also one of God's people and so he actively participates as an actor, but in addition to this he is a stagehand for God. He arranges the furniture and things like that. One of the pastor's biggest problems is to get out of the way when God pulls the curtain and the drama begins.

The second reason for a pastor is that he has time to do this work. Not all of God's people have the time to devote to spiritual work, but the pastor is paid to devote his time to it. Now, it is true that in doing this work full time, a pastor may find ways to function with great effectiveness. Indeed, it is hoped that a pastor will become an expert in the care of souls, so that he might share with his people the blessings God has given him. This is also the justification for a thorough seminary training, provided, of course, that the seminary one attends is not a torturous obstacle course on the road to spirituality. Even this, however, can be overcome by Him who leads the church, so long as our aspiring pastor surrenders himself and his time to the Lord. A man with time, working under the Holy Spirit, can do untold good for the kingdom of God by organizing the forms and structures for the new life under the Spirit, by listening to people and counseling them and by being, not an erudite scholar, but an obedient pupil of God. And, of course, a pastor has time to participate as an ordinary member of any small-group-church the Lord has raised up through his efforts.

It is through the small group, the essential church, that God and our fellow Christians break through to us, causing our loneliness to die. We become knit together—each brother and sister with the Lord. When a brother speaks to another in a small group, he listens for the voice of the Lord speaking through him. He takes his family seriously. They can teach him and he is accepted as a wise counselor by others in a wonderful experience of mutuality. There is an equality and a sharing which is very close, very precious. Our souls feel warmed as we gather with others around God. The loneliness is gone. We experience life together.

15. The life which is really living

> But what astonishes me . . . is the prodigious effect a real confession can have. Very often it is not only the decisive religious experience of freedom from guilt, but . . . the sudden cure of a physical or psychological illness. Sometimes in less than an hour there occurs in a patient, which I am seeing for the first time and to whom I have spoken but a few words, a release from psychological tension which I should have been very proud to obtain after months of therapy.[1]
>
> *Paul Tournier*

Anxiety, loneliness, unteachableness, conflict, possessiveness—are a few of our sorrows when we are self-enthroned.

The way out of our misery is to make our peace with God. No more climbing on His throne. No more playing god. No more self-enthronement.

It is time to descend from the throne of our hearts and confess our ultimate sin—pride which vaunts itself against God—to the Lord Jesus Christ who made "peace by the blood of his cross" (Colossians 1:20). God the Father, who patiently endures the humiliation of our quixotic assaults against His royal rule, is reunited with estranged mankind through the finished work of the Mediator, Jesus Christ.

Fully accept that, and we will cease being pretenders to the throne of our hearts. We will understand that we are *human,* that He is *divine,* and that there is a difference between the two. God is King. We are His subjects who find no indignity nor feel any resentment in this status because we accept ourselves as human persons and God as the Divine Person. He is the Leader; we are the followers. He is the Potter; we are the clay. It feels right and

---

[1] *Guilt and Grace,* New York: Harper and Row, Inc., 1962, p. 203.

appropriate to be His clay. But such clay! Clay in the image of God with the breath of the Almighty in us. Clay which sings: "Oh how great is thy goodness which thou hast laid up for them that fear thee" (Psalm 31:19, KJV).

Let us specify a few of the changes which take place in the new man in Christ. A whole set of new attitudes are created in the new man—new attitudes toward God, himself and other people. Let us look at the shape of that new, abundant life which is *really* worth living.

It is easy and delightful to see the change of attitude toward God. The urge to compete with Him is finished. The new man in Christ no longer pretends to have the "divine" qualities which are supposed to give God a run for His money. That strong urge to live perfectionistically is now seen for what it really is—an insane attempt to compete with and exceed the Divine Perfections. Our deluded minds once believed that we were simply trying to do our best. How naïve! We were really trying to compete with God. It was our intent to be more-than-human—to match His Perfections with our perfectionism. But no longer, thank God.

Now we no longer pit our time against His eternity. We once did this by living more than a day at a time.

Nor is it necessary to compete for the ultimate position in the world. Our fantasy of being Number 1 is dying. God is first. We are second.

Aforetime, we had a deep desire to be worshiped. To be sure, we did not call it that, but what else can we call our incessant need to be universally admired? In the case of some of us, *everyone* had to like us. We could never say *no*—only *yes*. It is different now. The disapproval of some is accepted. Indeed, not even God is universally admired! And to think that we strived for such acceptance! What a relief to be done with such madness.

In the past, we were always "right." God is right so we wanted to be right. Old friends can testify how unmovable we were. We usually reserve the word *immutable* to apply to the attributes of God, but it was also our attribute in the days when we took God on. But that is now in the past. We now afford ourselves the luxury of changing our minds, of being mutable.

There was a day when we tried to be the judges of all the earth. Everyday was our Judgment Day, though God will have only one. We were the judges, dispensing vengeance in full measure to everyone against whom we had pitted ourselves. Not now. We praise God for this verse in the Holy Scriptures: "Vengeance is mine, I will repay, says the Lord" (Romans 12:19). What a pleasure it is to resign as the self-appointed Dispenser of Justice!

In the days of our "oldness" we felt as omnicompetent as God. We even presumed to make atonement for our sins. Thank God we are delivered from those miserable efforts at self-atonement. They were insults to the perfect atonement of Christ. He is now our righteousness and our peace.

Christ is also our Power. We have withdrawn from the contest between I-will power and Christ's Power. "Thy kingdom come." "Thy will be done." "Thine is the kingdom and the power...." These phrases in our Lord's Prayer now mean something to us.

Our prayer-life is vastly different. Formerly we prayed for God to give us strength to overcome our problems. This made God our assistant. This was God used in the service of our egoism. Now we ask only to accept and do *His* will. We ask to follow Him, trusting that He will be the power in these new lives. It has finally gotten through to us that there is a vast difference between saying "God give me strength," and "Lord, You are the power in my life."

It must also be mentioned that the new life brings the expression of joy and gratitude into our prayers. Over and over, we find ourselves saying, "Thank You, Lord. We praise You." Some of us are surprised to find ourselves going back to singing and whistling—music-making for which we had no time nor feeling before the Light broke in on us. Now the whole world is lit up. It all looks so miraculous, so good! We affirm all of life. We love God.

And finally, our idea of freedom has changed. We once wanted to do as we wished, free to do anything. This is a freedom only God enjoys, but we also wanted it. No longer. We rejoice now in the proper use of our freedom—freedom to surrender and thereby win the victory.

By surrendering our aspirations to divinity, a wonderful calm and tranquility enters our souls. It is such a relief to stop pretending. We really became sick unto death of trying to play a part for which we were never intended. We miscast ourselves. On the day one finally walks off the stage of his life, hopefully never again to play god, on that day, peace of soul flows into the heart of that man with the silence and strength of an ocean tide.

So much for the abundant life in relationship to God. Observe the change in the positioned person in relationship to himself.

1. The major change I observe on this score is that *a person becomes free to begin and cease.* We have already discussed this at some length in Chapter 9. I wish only to add that being free does not always mean being a saint. Think, for example, of an alcoholic person who has found freedom from the bondage of his addiction. God has freed the man but he still has a long way to go. It may be that this man will have a "slip." His life may be in chaos in many

areas. He may, at times, be a very mixed-up fellow. Yet if sobriety has become a way of life to him, we must conclude that he is a free man who has momentarily slipped into bondage. Since sobriety is his way of life, however, we would expect to see improvement and victory in many areas other than alcoholism. It seems, however, that we become free by degrees. This is not difficult to understand when we recall that we also surrender to God by degrees. There is, of course, a direct correlation between surrender and freedom.

2. The positioned person also *asks new questions about himself*. The old questions, which could not but be faulty because they were formed by a mind distorted by egoistic mispositioning, were usually twofold: (a) *Why* did this problem happen to me? and (b) *How* did this problem begin? Both questions deal with etiology—the causal factors in the troubled life. The former question often leads to a conclusion that God "has it in for me," or it may lead to an "answer" as far out as astrology; or possibly a conviction that one is basically a defective and bad person. Such conclusions are sheer nonsense. The question "how" frequently sends the suffering person into a frantic, morbid investigation of his past history in which he supposedly locates the initial cause of his present problem. It is a fact, however, that even if the real roots of a problem could be found (which is highly doubtful in most cases), little profit comes from a mere revelation of causal factors. In spite of this, the unanswerable questions of *why* and *how* are obsessively put by the mispositioned person.

Positioning under God discards these old questions and focuses now on an appropriate, answerable and useful question—*Tell me how I can be helped?* To be sure, this question should be put to the right people—correctly positioned people, for only they can speak from an enlightened perspective. But notice how this question has a completely different tone to it. The new question comes from a teachable person—one who is ready to listen to a wisdom superior to his own, who is apparently ready to act on terms other than his own. He is ready for something bigger than himself. The old questions on the other hand, have already reached a conclusion as to what help is. "Help" is to answer *my* questions. They are usually asked in an insistent, defiant way, as if to say, "I want these questions answered before I budge one inch from where I now stand."

Wrong questions can only lead to the wrong answers. Thank God for the new question on our lips. God placed it there. It is the right question. It can lead to a right answer.

3. The positioned person is also marked, I have observed, by *a*

reversal of his priorities in life. Let us list the priority system of a mispositioned person.

First priority: *the hated "weakness" we enjoy.* You name it—alcohol, sex, money, neurosis, overeating, physical illness, clothes, drugs, compulsive gambling, education, power, pleasure, etc.

Second priority: *one's work.* One must work and earn money to support and find time for the "weakness."

Third priority: *the house.* A house is a place to sleep. Motels, because of the expense, impinge on the exercise of the weakness.

Fourth priority: *altruism.* By that we mean acts of kindness, particularly toward those who share our "weakness." These are drinking buddies in the case of alcoholics. Such people often come before the needs of our own family.

Fifth priority: *the children.* The young must be helped and protected, but not at the expense of higher priorities.

Sixth priority: *the spouse.* The spouse must always "live for the children." Children come first in the marriage; the spouse is second.

Seventh priority: *personal health* of body and mind. If there is any time, energy or money left over after the higher priorities are met, he will seek medical care, counsel, dental work, etc. Even lower in value than this is a program of spiritual care.

Eighth priority: *God,* last and least. I did not say *church.* Many of us have learned how to take our "weaknesses" right into church and feel very pious because of it. I said *God.*

The abundant life of a positioned person is built on a priority system quite the opposite of the above. It looks like this.

First priority: *God.* Now involvement in the church also makes sense. God is Highest Power. Everything else is dropped for His sake. He is number one.

Second priority: a program of *spiritual recovery.* After that, *health* of body and mind. The priorities which follow cannot be carried out unless the person is in a healthy state. To an alcoholic, this means that sobriety comes first after God.

Third priority: *the spouse.* Now the marriage. Children come after the needs of the marriage are met. Parents who live only for their children misposition themselves and ruin their children.

Fourth priority: *children.* Children should come to understand that the love of father and mother for each other holds their marriage together rather than their devotion to their children.

Fifth priority: helpful *service* to the larger family of mankind. Compassion and altruism toward all of God's children should always come before the "things" that follow.

Sixth priority: *a home.* A home is some sort of building wherein to express our love of persons. The home need not be pretentious. It may even lack good plumbing, but it is still a home if the people in it have love in their hearts.

Seventh priority: *the job.* Blessed is the man who can let his job come and go without falling apart. What we do for a living is not nearly so important as we think. Remember that in three generations, hardly anyone will know what we did. In fact, after four generations, it is doubtful that our own offspring will remember our names!

Eighth priority: *the hated "weakness"* we enjoy. Hopefully, it will never get any attention.

4. The positioned person is also marked by *a paradoxical style of life.* Bruce Larson mentions four of these paradoxes:
(a) We surrender to win.
(b) We must give away to keep.
(c) We have to suffer to get well.
(d) We have to die to live.[2]
In a very real sense, these four points are a declaration of our new freedom and also new rights. We are now free to surrender, free to die to self, free to suffer and free to share. The bondage is gone. New freedom has given us new rights.

I vividly recall a meeting with my pastor in which I was bemoaning the difficult set of problems I was facing. I also complained about his rather bold advice on how to meet them. Somewhat in desperation, I concluded my complaints by asking, with

[2] Larson, *Living on the Growing Edge,* Grand Rapids: Zondervan Publishing House, 1968, p. 47.

considerable feeling: "What am I going to do?" To this the pastor had a quiet answer: "I give you the right to suffer." When I recovered from the blast of his whispered words, I realized that he was right. I had not given myself such a right. After that, I felt better, though I did suffer.

5. Finally, the new man in Christ is blessed with a *new set of attitudes,* of which I would like to mention just four:

a. Humility. It is a virtue which no man can achieve. It is a gift from God. The recipient of this gift is largely unaware of it. Others, however, notice that the phoniness, the gaseous qualities, the egocentricity are dying. The new man emerging is much more the man he simply is. He is real. He lives in truth, abhorring self-debasement as much as self-exaltation.

b. Teachableness. We can now learn from others—indeed, from all men. It is no longer necessary to always teach, always striving to get our point across, often by breaking down the points of others. Hopefully, we can learn even from our peers. It is a glorious freedom not always to know it all. Unfortunately, most modern knowledge is used by people to compete against each other. The positioned man simply says: "No contest."

c. Contentment. The new man under God is at peace. The war is over. The surrendered man now lives under the will of God, accepting what He gives, continually "squaring off" for what the good Lord provides. The cup mentioned in Psalm 23 finally overflows. One is then ready to really live. A wonderful affirmation of life follows! The world looks good. Our negative screen through which we had viewed the world is removed.

Concomitant with the affirmation of life is a paradoxical willingness to die, when God so wills it. This is not a death wish. It is an acceptance of the Father's wise plan. Even our Brother, Jesus Christ, passed through death. It is appropriate that we follow Him. At the Father's choosing, we will leave time and enter eternity. Time really does not matter too much any more and as its importance fades, one suddenly understands why Christ called the new life eternal.

d. Joy. Dethroned people who have enthroned God have joy. It is interior joy. Outwardly there may be much pain and sadness, but one can still locate the presence of that inward treasure which causes us to be filled with joy. It is so real, at times, that it will cause a person to quietly sit in his chair and smile, radiating that joy. At other times we find ourselves singing. I often wonder, too, whether the phenomenon of speaking in tongues, both in the early church and today, is not a way of expressing this deep, almost unspeakable joy.

Finally, let us consider the fruit of ego-dethronement in relation to our fellows. Consider three matters.

1. *The correctly positioned person aborts his anger.* Anger (which means that we live *over* a person to judge him and *against* a person to destroy him) aborts itself when a person lives *under* God and *with* people. There is no need, theoretically, for a positioned person to express his anger because it does not come to birth. To be sure, none of us reaches this degree of perfection, for in actual life we jump on the throne all too often. I am sure, too, that once anger comes to birth in our emotional life, it is often better to express it in nondestructive ways than to repress or suppress it.

A much more important point, however, is to understand that as anger aborts in a positioned person, an attitude of compassion comes to birth. It is this attitude which now characterizes the new man. He feels with and for people, even those who do him wrong. The need to resent and oppose is replaced by love.

This opens the door to nonviolence and nonretaliation as a way of life, as our Lord taught us. As egoists, we are violent, retaliatory people, usurping from the Almighty the function of executing judgment. Living under God will free us to be compassionate when we are wronged without cause.

2. *Fear is dissipated.*

When one is afraid he feels endangered by superior destructive forces in the face of which he feels helpless. Faith in God withers up fear. Faith in oneself or in other people causes a rank growth of fear to grow.

The fears of a mispositioned person usually cluster around people because people are the primary threat, he feels, to his ultimate position as number one in his world. He feels *under* and *against* people and therefore, afraid of them. Fear is the reverse of anger where one feels *over* and *against*. These two feelings are actually the closest brothers, alternately ruling the person; recall that the mispositioned person lives under the tyranny of his feelings.

We should note here that when anger goes out as a way of life, fear goes with it and *vice versa*. Picture anger as a nine-foot tall man in us and fear as a three-foot tall man. In reality, we are six feet, let us say. When the anger-man is reduced to the reality of six feet, the fear man simultaneously grows to the reality of six feet. The positioned person is one who consciously lives in the reality that he is six feet, no more and no less.

We say, in the case of anger, that one can forego the temptation to become angry if (1) he leaves vengeance in the hands of the Lord and (2) chooses to follow the advice of Christ to express compassion and love toward others. The same principles apply to fear. The tyrannical feeling of fear can be repulsed by (1) direct appeal to God to be *the* power (which is different from asking God to help *us*) and a faith which abandons ourselves to His strength and (2) choosing to work co-operatively *with* people, expressing love for them in concrete ways.

Fear aborts when love is conceived. "There is no fear in love, but perfect love casts out fear. For fear has to do with punishment, and he who fears is not perfected in love" (I John 4:18).

3. The new man in Christ displays an additional unique characteristic and with the mention of it, I wish to conclude this book, for it seems to me a worthy point on which to end. God's newly positioned man is a person who loses interest in the question *Who is right?*

In the old style of life, the egoist lived argumentatively. He would take others on, pitting his "right answers" against their errors. This meant, of course, that the egoist would work hard at concealing his errors and would openly display his "truth," for how else could he be adjudged as right?

The ethic of Christ changes all that, for He teaches us to conceal the glorious story of how right we are and to confess where we are wrong. Our Lord gives us the right to be wrong and to be known as such. Our need, then, to be judgmental dissipates.

The old question is supplanted by a new, meaningful statement: *By the grace of God, I, who was dead, now live.* It is, in its best expression, a quiet declaration to whoever cares to listen, that a light has been turned on in a miserably darkened life; that a food has finally been found which really gives strength; that a drab and meaningless existence has ended and a wonderfully exciting life has begun.

This new, living person is now able to testify to the miracle that God has worked in him. That testimony is often scorned by those who endlessly raise questions and reject those who claim to have found an answer. And let's face it—sometimes God's people do exude a feeling of superiority because they have an answer which others lack. There are still others who hear the declaration of what God has done in a particular life as a throwback to an old-style religious testimony of the revival tent meeting. Old stereotypes and inappropriate sensationalism notwithstanding, the modern method of effective help for troubled people seems to be through the hope aroused and light given when a genuine testimony is spoken of God's power in a life. Witness the effectiveness of the Anonymous groups (Alcoholics, Narcotics, Neurotics, Schizophrenics, Gamblers) and the phenomenal growth of the *Faith at Work* movement in the churches. All employ the testimonial approach. All testify to a problem and a program to get out of the problem. All point to God as the answer. They say, "But for the grace of God. . . ." All encourage others who may be ready for help to try God.

Those who are helped by God will be understandably thrilled about it. And why should they not then share God with others who may be ready for Him? This new-found treasure is not just for God's new man. God is for all. The rightly positioned person understands that he is not the end-point of God's grace. God's way is that each one reach one. Indeed, if the treasure is not shared, we lose God and our new style of life with Him. So we give away to keep.

This brings God's power into our lives.

And great joy.

Peace.

But even better, we need be god-players no longer.

We have found—or did He find us?—the One whom we have really been seeking all these years.

God.

APPENDICES

Appendix A
"In the Middle, Einstein"

*(From a tape recording of a speech given by
Allen G. at an Alcoholics Anonymous Banquet.[1])*

My name is Allen G. I am an alcoholic. In the beginning, I was a working drunk but not because I was a career man. I had no income, no annuities, no rich relatives, but I had a thirst. In order to drink, I had to have money and in order to get money, I had to suffer the indignities of labor. I always found myself in positions that were very much beneath my dignity. I was always subject to the supervision of people whom I regarded as intellectual peasants.

The period Monday through Friday was for me a very unpleasant interlude between drinking. But inevitably, Friday would arrive and about noontime, I would begin to experience a very pleasant glow of anticipation. I hadn't had a drink yet, but already I was beginning to fly. I would force myself, semi-hysterically, through those last four hours of Friday. Finally, it was 4:30—the blessed time. I now faced the week end. For the alcoholic, it is amazing when he views a week end prospectively from Friday, what an interminable period of time it is. Here I am—my own boss. *Nobody can push me around.* And I have *money.* This is indeed the best of all possible worlds!

I would first take myself home and go through the motions of having dinner. Immediately thereafter, I would get meticulously attired. In all my sartorial elegance, I would walk two blocks, turn in at the local gin-mill, ascend a stool and give forth with the erudition. Usually on my left hand was the local garbage collector; on my right hand, the neighborhood iceman; in the middle,

---

[1] Used with the author's permission.

Einstein. There was no subject on which I was not an expert. The conversations were tremendous, stimulating, all-encompassing. Very quickly they progressed to the point where everybody talked, nobody listened, nobody gave a damn. Then, all too quickly came that inevitable time: the guy who owned the joint wanted to go home. There would then ensue the inevitable argument—one for the road. This I insisted upon. This I needed like a hole in the head. This I would get.

I would then take myself very unsteadily home, crawl up the stairs into the sack and collapse. There would follow four or five hours of alcoholic stupor. I would awaken, Saturday morning—sick, bad taste, butterflies in the stomach, but with an awareness: *This is Saturday.*

"All right, so you are a little sick. The joints are still open. You still have money, so this morning luxuriate in your misery." We would then stretch out for an additional hour. Then we would arise, and once again, meticulously attired, two blocks, same gin-mill, same stool, same characters, same conversation, same results: 2 P.M. —stiff! Back into the sack, unconscious. At 5 P.M., awake, sick, but it is *still* Saturday. Don't worry. Double-header today.

So right back again, two blocks, same stool, all things the same. At 3 A.M. Sunday, same bartender, same argument: one for the road. Come 3:30, I would crawl up the same stairs. Back into the sack. Collapse. Then four or five hours of alcoholic stupor. Now it's Sunday morning. I am awake, sick. No butterflies this morning— *eagles* this morning. Also an awareness that this is Sunday. Tomorrow is Monday. The week end has telescoped. Tomorrow we must earn the daily bread. Tomorrow we must hit the ball. And we know that our string is running out. We can feel the hot breath on the neck. How many grandparents can you bury? How many attacks of spastic colitis can you have—always on Monday?

We know that the job is slipping and that we need the job. We want to keep the job but right now we have an immediate problem—we are sick. But we are also intelligent. All alcoholics are geniuses. So we use this. We shall program this day. Point One: recovery. This we know how to do. Be home at 2 P.M. Stay home. Don't go out tonight. Back to bed early. Eight hours of sleep. Tomorrow morning: on our feet early. Hit the ball. No hits, no runs, no errors. This is our program.

We arise. As we sally forth, we execute Point One brilliantly. By 2 P.M.—blind! By 2:30 P.M., back into the sack, unconscious. By 5 P.M., awake, suffering. But we remember the resolve of this morning. We are further aware of the closer proximity of Monday. We want to keep this resolve. And now we begin to prowl from room to room like a caged tiger. The perspiration begins to flow. The nerves begin to dance. Finally, we throw up our hands and say: "Who the hell am I kidding? If I put my head down on a pillow tonight, it will explode. Just a few beers—so I can sleep."

So back to the same stool. And again, all things are the same. It is 2 A.M. Monday. Same bartender, same argument: one for the road. At 2:30 A.M., back into the sack, unconscious. Now it is Monday and I'm going to die. I sit on the edge of the bed, head between the hands, the perspiration cascading down my face. Every nerve is quivering. And then, the self-loathing begins— "What kind of a fool *are* you? *Why* must you always stay until the last shot is fired? Oh, God!" The only time we communicate with Deity—Monday morning.

The little lady stands over the bed and she shakes her head from side to side in perplexity. I say to her: "Please, not this morning. Leave me alone." And then, with terrific effort, we drag the quivering wreck from the soggy bed. We stumble into our clothes, aim ourselves in the direction of employment. Every step is purgatory. Finally, at long last, we get to the entrance of our place of employment and stumble through the gate. And here come the normal ones. "Good morning!" (said in a happy falsetto voice). You want to *kill* 'em. We stumble into an office and grope our way to a desk where we select a nondescript piece of correspondence. For eight hours, we carry it like a banner from office to office. "Please God, don't let anybody ask me any questions which require an intelligent answer today. Please God, make it 4:30 quick." This is prayer.

And finally, at long last, the blessed time 4:30 arrives. The wounded warrior returns home. The little woman is happy to see you but you say: "No questions, please. Just let me die." Back into the sack. Twice that night the sheets come off the bed. We are bathed in our own perspiration.

Finally, it is Tuesday. It's not much better. For eight hours, we cheat, chisel, and connive our way through the boss's time. Then, back home and right into the sack. Now it is Wednesday. About 8:30 A.M. Wednesday, we have the first manifestations of health returning because right about then, we begin to notice around us the existence of certain small inefficiencies in the corporation. Wednesday night, returning home, we have the semblance of a spring in the step and we announce to the little woman that tonight the master is taking sustenance. "Let me have a bullion cube and a cup of hot water."

Then it is Thursday and by 9 A.M. Thursday, we are convinced of one thing—the entire population of this corporation save one are imbeciles! You have to show them how to do everything. On Thursday night, we demand lamb chops, broiled.

Finally, it's noontime Friday and here's that old feeling again. At 4:30 it's week end again and here's money and we are on our way home. But we are not completely insensible people. We have a vivid recollection of the week that has just concluded. We are aware of the small kindnesses extended by the little woman. She was not such a bad skate. She didn't use the spurs too hard this week. But there is also a gnawing realization which says: "I got to get out!" but we'll worry about that later.

Into the house we come. It's immaculate and the kids are scrubbed and shining. A nice dinner is on the table. Even the wife looks pretty good. These are all the wrong ingredients, so being alcoholic, we go on the prowl. We go from room to room and ultimately discover one household chore which did not get attention that day. We say to the little woman: "What happened?"

"I was busy."

"So, you were busy. Did you see me, a dying man, leave this house every morning this week to keep a roof over your head, and you can't take care of a simple detail like this?" This type of needling eventually evokes a response. The minute she answered me back, she was dead.

"You don't appreciate me!" I shouted.

Out we go and we're heading right back to the stool. Right about here an interesting conflict begins to manifest itself. On one level of the alleged intelligence, we have just put over a sharp deal. Nice going. But on another level, way down deep, there is a little voice which intrudes itself and says: "She did not deserve it and you know it, you phony bum!" But this voice I can't listen to now. Let me get back to the stool. Let me have a few and I'll figure out a way to square it later. Also, we have a vivid recollection of Monday which has just gone by. Don't let that happen again. Just stick to beer. Get out of that joint at a reasonable hour. You can do it. Watch it.

The week end begins. It goes by and again it's Monday. It's different—it's worse!

This is my case history, except as with every practicing alcoholic, it got progressively worse. It came to a point where it was no longer possible to go to work on Monday, nor on Tuesday, nor the other days of the week. But I was able to escape into the armed services during World War II.

In 1945, I stood before His Honor in a courtroom, as do most practicing alcoholics. To put it charitably, I was placed under supervision in the bastille. Out of this encounter, I heard my first reference to

Alcoholics Anonymous. His Honor looked me over and said: "Well, I see you're a veteran." I had on the ruptured duck we used to wear at that time. "You are quite a young punk. If I were you, I would contact Alcoholics Anonymous."

I said "Yes sir" to him and to myself, "You should drop dead, Your Honor." But regardless, I went to the bastille and I did not care for the cuisine, the accommodations, nor the associations. I wanted out, so I wrote a letter and nothing happened. Finally, my good wife relented and got me released on my second son's birthday. I went to live at the home of my parents. My father is a retired policeman—not too sympathetic. I spent my Thanksgiving Day in his home. He spent his time glaring at me. Finally, there came a knock at the door and there was a guy who held up a letter. "Did you write this?"

"Yes," I said, "but who needs you now? I'm out of prison." But he was a persistent character, eventually wearing me down and so it was that I went to my first AA meeting. I went primarily to get away from the baleful glance of my father. Here I received my introduction to AA. The only ingredient I had was quiet desperation. I had no home, no job, poor health, no money, no friends, no self-respect. I had no prospects, I had nothing! Now if this hoople wanted to take me in his car at his expense to an AA meeting—why not? It was a night out.

I sat and listened to the speakers at AA. Every time they split an infinitive, I was wounded! I had this supreme arrogance of the Irish alcoholic. But this arrogance worked in my favor because I evaluated the mental caliber of the protagonists there. I figured that if these hooples could stay sober with this mumbo jumbo, well, for me, it's got to be a cinch. So, on the basis of a challenge, I said: "I'll show them." I continued to go to meetings. This challenge motivation was perfect for me because I did one thing right—I did not drink. For all the wrong reasons, but I did not drink. Days became weeks and weeks became months. My wife said: "Whatever it is, keep *doing* it!"

Six months and I still had not had a drink. Then one of those situations developed where there was a meeting scheduled and the visiting group did not show up. We had a frantic chairman galloping around the room. "Have to rig a meeting." He turned to me and said: "How long you been sober?"

"Six months," I said.

"Talk!" Now this is not the way to approach an alcoholic. Since I was the novice, when the meeting began, I was speaker Number One.

When I got up on my feet, I said: "My name is Allen G. I am an alcoholic." This was important. This was the first public admission. Why not? It didn't cost me a nickel. I had seen others do it, so why not me? This was an admission for their benefit. I said, "I am an alcoholic. I've been coming around here for six months. I've been looking for peace and serenity until I'm left-handed. *Where the hell is it?"*

Then I sat down.

That was the quietest room in New Jersey. When the meeting was over, I was surrounded. One very casual little guy by the name of Grant, came sauntering up to me and said: "Come here, Hot Shot." He said: "I have observed you for six months and I do believe that you have been sober. I have seen you here every week. Now apparently from those few little gems that you gave out with tonight, during this period, some things have been troubling you. Then, one question—Why, didn't you *say* something about it?" This was a fair question and I didn't have an answer. I had rather been found dead.

I went back home that night and went to bed. I tossed, turned and went through that Danny Thomas routine,—"I should've said . . . I should've said" . . . . nothing. The guy was right.

So next week I went back and selected a small nucleus of the intelligentsia to whom I unburdened myself somewhat. This was progress. And I did not drink. By virtue of the simple process of not taking alcohol, things began to happen of their own volition. I stopped shaking, I stopped sweating. I began to eat. I got a job. I got a suit, coat and pants to match. I got a dollar. My head began to come up and I liked the feeling! More important, I began to listen not so critically.

I also began to recognize that these case histories to which I am being exposed week after week, were nothing more or less than the simple projection of the basic symptoms of alcoholism. I had to admit that if these were the symptoms of alcoholism, these were *my* symptoms. So I must be an alcoholic, I reasoned. I had progressed from the qualified admission for their benefit to a reluctant acceptance of the label. " 'All right, I'll buy it. I'm an alcoholic. I'll buy it for now."

Arrogance was far from dead, though. "Give me a year. Give me one solid year without a drink. Give me this year to repair my financial fences. Give me this year to become revitalized, physically, spiritually, economically, emotionally. Give me a year to get back into the business world. Give me the knowledge that I have gained by my association with these characters and I'll show them!" But I had accepted temporarily the label—and time went by. Seven, eight, nine months and I got to know more and more people.

I also began to observe the very unhappy "experiment department." This is something to watch. . . . Never once did I observe the successful experiment. Every one ended disastrously. And when I began to measure these guys against me with their obvious superiority in every department, I began to wonder—*Is a year going to be enough?* Now I've progressed to the point of conviction. This means me for keeps, and I don't like it! Here I am—age thirty-three—and I love those neon signs. I got a lot of mileage left in me. *Why* does this have to happen to me? I moaned and I groaned.

One day my little casual buddy said, "Come here, Hot Shot. I'm listening to you and you sound like a wounded moose. You're always crying. There's a word that requires some attention with you. The word is *surrender*."

And now I had him. I turned on my tormentor and said: "Wait a minute, boy. When I came in here, you guys said you take what you want. You don't have to do anything. Is that true?"

Yes, it was true.

"Now when you tell me I must surrender, to this logical mind this implies that I must surrender to something. To me, this sounds like a tambourine, and I ain't gonna buy it. I have a year on *my* basis. Who the hell says I have to be happy?"

Only an alcoholic could construct a gem of logic like that. But this cookie was smart because he said: "Okay, kid, have it your own way, but keep coming."

In addition to this casual counselor, I also had a sponsor. This man was the soul of patience and kindness. With me, he had to be. About this stage of my development, it seemed that every week end, my sponsor's little Chevrolet would come chugging into my driveway. John would say: "Come on."

"Where am I going?"

"So what's the difference? You have nothing else to do. Get in."

The first occasion, we took off to a neighboring town, pulled up to a house, knocked on the door and a woman came to the door. She looked beat. She said: "Are you from AA?"

"That's right."

"Well, it's upstairs."

I ascended the stairs with John. I did not know what I was getting into until I opened the bedroom door and then I knew. Here lay the pigeon. He was shaking. The bed was shaking. The room was shaking. Old John says to me: "Go sit in the corner. Be quiet."

John sat next to this pigeon and began to talk—not about the pigeon but about John: the way he drank; the way he schemed; the way he connived; the way he got into AA. And as John was talking to this character, it was amazing to observe that the bed began to quiet down and the guy begins nodding his head: "Yeah . . . Yeah . . . Gee . . . Gee . . ." And I'm fascinated! I figure this guy John is a magician. He's got to be!

Finally, John puts it to him—the $64 question: "You want to quit? Yeah? When? Now? Okay, Let's go to a meeting." Bingo. In the space of a few short weeks this horizontal character is a *man.* I'm amazed by the prowess of John! It seemed every week we were off—pigeons here, pigeons there. I was always super cargo— "Go to the corner. Sit down. Shut up."

Finally I got to that place of material affluence where we got a four-party telephone. On this particular day, it rang. I picked up the phone and there was my friend, John, saying: "Allen, there's a guy over in Keansburg who wants help." This is a nearby community.

I say, "Well, are you going?"

He says, "I can't make it."

Well, I know what's coming. I said, "Well, that's tough. Too bad I can't help you, John, because I haven't got a car."

"But where I'm going, I'll not use the car, so suppose you take it."

My first emotion was panic. I didn't want any part of this deal. Who is this clown in Keansburg? I never saw him. He never saw me. Why should I drop dead for him? I don't want to go.

Yet, something else intruded itself here. This was my sponsor, John, who had been nothing but the soul of kindness, patience and tolerance with me. This was the first request he had ever made of me. How could I, in good conscience, refuse John?

"So what do you think? Can you handle it?"

"Sure." So I took the car and went to the house.

"I'm from AA. Where is he?"

"It's upstairs." I go in. Same picture. Horizontal. Shakes. I must begin. What am I going to tell this character? Well, I saw John operate. John used to tell them about John. So I told him—this is the way I drank; this is the way I operated; this is what happened to me. In the right places, I am getting the right responses. This is terrific! I got a warm feeling inside me. I like this guy! This guy will get AA if I have to kill him!

So I poured it on. Finally we got to the strategic point—You want to quit? Yes. When? Now. Okay. Be ready. I will be here Monday. Down the stairs I went. His wife grabbed me.

"Can I see you?"

"Yes ma'am," In the kitchen I got a two-hour recitation on what a louse he was. This guy is completely out of business. He owes everybody. He is unemployable. He's out.

"What am I going to do?" she asked.

I have the answer. "Easy does it!"

Finally, there came the appointed night. I was there early. He was there, vertical, ambulatory. "Get in." Off we went to the meeting. We came through the door and like a homing pigeon, he went for the last seat, last row.

I told him, "Uhh, uhh. Up front. I don't want you to miss anything." So up we came and sat in the first row. The meeting began. The speakers got up—and they said everything wrong. Here I was next to my pigeon. I wanted this guy to get AA. "Come on! Get *to* it! Get off the travelogue and get on AA." I was sweating blood. I turned to look at my pigeon. He was like a rock.

What is this picture all about? There I sat with a guy I had seen only once before. But about this guy I knew everything. His wife told me. There I sat intensely interested in this man—for *his* sake. This was the first division of concentration on self in a lifetime. There I sat, intensely interested in another human being, and from this relationship I could not make a nickel. He didn't have one. But this relationship was real. It was valid. You could see it. We were together. This human relationship of one alcoholic for the other was completely devoid of any material aspects. Yet it existed. There was the militant agnostic. There was the guy who was embarrassed by God references. And there he sat, engaged in the practice of spirituality and too dumb to know it!

These things I recite only in the interest of the individual who might be sitting here tonight, who is apprehensive about not understanding what is entailed in this program of AA. Don't worry about it. Just come in as I did. Go through the motions. Do what is suggested. Don't drink. Continue to make these meetings. Get to know some of the people and you will discover a progression in AA as there was progression in your alcoholism. Those things which confuse, perplex and bewilder you will clear up. You only have to do one thing. Don't take one drink this day. And keep coming to these meetings. Place your faith in people first, if necessary. Utlimately, you will find that you can place your faith in God. This is your own selection. One day at a time—one Friend, one belief, one faith, one life restored.

Appendix B
The Twelve Steps

(Here follows the Twelve Steps of Alcoholics Anonymous. There are only two references to alcohol in the Steps. Note that in both cases, they are not essential to the content. People with other problems, such as narcotics and gambling, are finding the Steps also work for them. It is the thesis of this book that (1) all people are afflicted with serious, defeating problems and (2) that steps such as these offer a spiritual program which goes in the direction of recovery and victory.)

1. We admitted we were powerless over alcohol, that our lives had become unmanageable.
2. Came to believe that a Power greater than ourselves could restore us to sanity.
3. Made a decision to turn our will and our lives over to the care of God *as we understood Him.*
4. Made a searching and fearless moral inventory of ourselves.
5. Admitted to God, to ourselves, and to another human being the exact nature of our wrongs.
6. Were entirely ready to have God remove all these defects of character.
7. Humbly asked Him to remove our shortcomings.
8. Made a list of all persons we had harmed, and became willing to make amends to them all.
9. Made direct amends to such people wherever possible, except when to do so would injure them or others.
10. Continued to take personal inventory and when we were wrong promptly admitted it.
11. Sought through prayer and meditation to improve our conscious contact with God *as we understood Him* praying only for knowledge of His will for us and the power to carry that out.

12. Having had a spiritual awakening as the result of those steps we tried to carry this message to alcoholics and to practice these principles in all our affairs.[1]

---

[1] Alcoholics Anonymous Fellowship, *Twelve Steps and Twelve Traditions*, 1953.

Appendix C

Private Confession in the Cure of Souls
by John Calvin

"Scripture, moreover, approves . . . of private confession '. . . confess your sins to one another, and pray for one another . . .' (James 5:16). For James means that, disclosing our weaknesses to one another, we help one another with mutual counsel and consolation . . . even though James, by not expressly determining on whose bosom we should unburden ourselves, leaves us free choice to confess to that one of the flock of the church who seems most suitable. Yet we must also preferably choose pastors inasmuch as they should be judged especially qualified above the rest. Now I say that they are better fitted than the others because the Lord has appointed them by the very calling of the ministry to instruct us by word of mouth to overcome and correct our sins, and also to give us consolation through assurance of pardon (Matthew 16:19; 18:18; John 20:23). For, while the duty of mutual admonition and rebuke is entrusted to all Christians, it is especially enjoined upon ministers. Thus, although all of us ought to console one another and confirm one another in assurance of divine mercy, we see that the ministers themselves have been ordained witnesses and sponsors of it to assure our consciences of forgiveness of sins, to the extent that they are said to forgive sins and to loose souls. When you hear that this is attributed to them, recognize that it is for your benefit.

"Therefore, let every believer remember that, if he be privately troubled and afflicted with a sense of sins, so that without outside help he is unable to free himself from them, it is a part of his duty not to neglect what the Lord has offered to him by way of remedy. Namely, that, for his relief, he should use private confession to his own pastor; and for his solace, he should beg the private help of him whose duty it is, both publicly and privately, to comfort the people of God by the gospel teaching.

". . . I do not so much object to sheep presenting themselves to their shepherd as often as they wish to partake of the Sacred

Supper; rather, I ardently wish this to be observed everywhere. For both those who have an encumbered conscience can thence receive a remarkable benefit and those who should be admonished may thus be prepared for admonitions, provided tyranny and superstition be always excluded."[1]

---

[1] John Calvin, *Institutes of the Christian Religion,* Book III, Chapter IV, Sections 12, 13. Edited by John T. McNeill, translated by Ford Lewis Battles. (Philadelphia: The Westminster Press, 1960).

APPENDIX D

QUESTIONS FOR DISCUSSION

A Study Guide for

Chapter 1: *Man Is Human Spirit*
1. Since this is our first meeting, let us go around our circle, each one stating his name and giving a brief biography.
2. What spoke to you in this first chapter?
3. The first chapter is about man as a choosing spirit. You have made a number of significant choices in your life. Let each one share the *wisest* choice in his personal history. Explain.
4. Choosing *for* something always implies a choice *against* something else. In your wisest choice, what did you choose against?
5. Close the meeting with prayer, going around the circle.

Chapter 2: *God's Astonishing Appraisal*
1. Let us begin by reacting to anything in this chapter which caught our interest.
2. Most modern people believe that we feel superior to others because we really feel inferior; that we hide these inferiority feelings by acting arrogantly and haughty. Can you share any episode from your life where you hid your *superiority* feelings by acting inferiorly?
3. Do you think God loves even those who insistently and defiantly oppose Him? Where and when does God's love end?
4. Sigmund Freud spoke of "His Majesty, the Baby." Someone else, a theologian, said that there is no room for God in a baby's thinking because a baby is so completely egocentric and self-concerned. Since the baby is in the center of his world, he is, in a sense, his own god. Later, the person will need to surrender this central place to God, if God is ever to become real to him. React to these statements.

Chapter 3: *The Self-Enthroned Egoist*
1. What spoke to you in this chapter?
2. The question whether man is basically good or basically

evil has long been debated. This chapter argues that God made man basically good but man is mis-positioned. That is, he stands in the wrong place, in God's place. This mis-positioning is sin, rather than some inherent evil in our make-up. How does all this sound to you?

3. "It would seem that health is a state granted to those who voluntarily live under authority whereas illness is a consequence of ultimatizing one's self in the world" (p. 35). Do you think in this way we might be said to earn our illnesses?

Chapter 4: *The Ultimatized Man*

1. Did you meet yourself in this chapter? Where particularly?

2. The last paragraph on page 43 describes something of what it feels like to have a nervous breakdown. Would you agree that everyone here has in some way and to some degree had a nervous breakdown? Perhaps the only thing that kept us from hospitalization was that we succeeded in being very quiet about the whole matter. Divulge to your friends here something of your last private nervous breakdown.

3. Turn to the verbatim account on pages 44 and 45. Would the two people to the right of the chairman each take a part and read this dialogue? Now go around with this question: Was the counselor's approach loving or rejective?

Chapter 5: *Living Against People*

1. React to any point that stirred you in this chapter.

2. You notice that I have precious little to say in favor of anger. One of my friends commented: "But surely there is a place for *righteous* anger!" I responded: "On the contrary! *That* is the *worst* kind because we then reek of sanctimony!" Where do your feelings lie in this conversation?

3. When was *the* time you erected your portable court-room and appointed yourself judge of a person who wasn't even around to defend himself? Explain.

Chapter 6: *Playing God*

1. React to the contents of this chapter.

2. E. Stanley Jones reports a troubled person who came to him saying: "I came to find myself. I'm a self-holic—I'm dedicated to myself even though others think I'm a very selfless person." Let us go around our group, if you are willing, each contributing—

   a. One current example from your life where you are a self-holic and,

   b. Turn to the person on your right and ask for his reaction and counsel.

3. One needs to decide, it seems to me, whether he is playing god or playing the child. If the problem is childishness, we will need to grow up in order to live. If the problem is "godishness," we will need to die in order to live. Since we cannot go in two directions at one time, a choice of direction is necessary. Which direction would you recommend?

Chapter 7: *Law and License*

1. React to any part of the chapter which spoke with some force to you.
2. Evaluate: Obeying the Ten Commandments is an empty religious gesture until one has resigned as his own god and come to terms with the Law-Giver.
3. Suppose someone said to you: "As long as I think something is right for me, it is perfectly all right to do it." Let each group member give his response to such a statement. (Check the author's response in the last three paragraphs of this chapter.)

Chapter 8: *The Action of Guilt*

1. You are driving alone on a seldom-used road in the desert. A stop sign comes into view. No one could possibly be around as you approach the intersection. Would you stop or ignore the sign? This situation raises some interesting questions:
   a. Do I obey the law only when my disobedience might be detected?
   b. Is God to be considered a watching authority in this situation?
   c. If I disobey the sign, will this result in a sense of guilt which, as it is internalized, will break me down?
   d. When does my personal authority supersede external authority?
   e. Must a law be reasonable before I obey it?
2. Ultimately, the action of guilt can be stopped only by forgiveness from both God and man. If a sense of guilt persists even after this forgiveness, would you see this kind of self-judgment as another form of playing god?

Chapter 9: *The Life of Bondage*

1. Let each member give an example of an area in his life where he has a problem in beginning ("My accelerator doesn't work!") and another where he has a problem in stopping ("My brakes do not work!").
2. "The way to become free is to lose our freedom." What this means is that the way to become a free-to-begin-and-

stop human being is to lose our freedom to do whatever *we* wish, becoming a freed slave of Jesus Christ. How does this sound to you?

3. When we speak of alcoholism (which is a problem in stopping) as a disease, we mean that it is out of control to stop, just as a head cold cannot be stopped. Does this mean that the alcoholic is helpless to do anything about his out-of-controlness? What can he do and what can he not do?

Chapter 10: *The Way of the Cross*

1. First, general reactions to this chapter.
2. What would you say—is it necessary for *all* people to experience "the way of the cross" in their lives?
3. Share whatever you wish of "the way of the cross" in your own life.
4. Read the fifth paragraph on page 99, beginning with: "It is for this reason . . ." do you feel this paragraph has any application to the task of raising our children?

Chapter 11: *The Death of Our Freedom*

1. This chapter can be summarized as follows: Those who try to be *in control,* go *out of control,* until they come *under control.* What does this mean to you?
2. There are those in our group who have concretely entered into the experience of inner freedom promised by Christ. Do share your experience and invite the reaction of others present.

Chapter 12: *The Death of Our Egoism*

1. Any general reactions to this chapter? How does this whole idea of confession strike you?
2. Please read the third paragraph on page 114 beginning with "Robert Raines tells us . . . ." He mentions his friend. Suppose you were that friend. How would you feel? Would you respond as this friend responded?
3. I have found it to be an ideal arrangement where two people, desiring to make confession to God, alternate in hearing each other's confession. I observe, also, that this arrangement works very well between laymen, no clergyman being needed. Finally, I have yet to see a breach of confidence among such people. How does all this sound to you?

Chapter 13: *The Death of Our Guilt*

1. Someone has said that the tone of this chapter is far more Roman Catholic than Protestant. What do you think?

2. Is there anything which stands in the way of your entering into the confessional arrangement suggested in this chapter? Let us go around the circle on this question. Do not seek unity with the ideas of others. Be frank and spontaneous.
3. Has anyone a report to bring about his experience with confession?

Chapter 14: *The Death of Loneliness*
1. Is there anything in this chapter which either frightens or angers you?
2. It is common to say that what a lonely person needs is the love and acceptance of his fellows. This is true, but it lets the lonely person off the hook too easily. What can the *loner* do? Let each member reflect on how he has handled his loneliness.
3. Is there, perhaps, a consensus that this might be the right time to organize small groups in your church? Excellent materials for beginning can be obtained from the Faith at Work Handbooks. Send $2.20 for eight different guides to Faith at Work, 4800 West Waco Dr., Waco, Texas 76703.

Chapter 15: *The Life Which Is Really Living*
1. I have an idea to which I would like your reaction. It is my conviction that the reason people reject the Gospel of Christ is because *the news is too good*. This chapter mentions only a few of the blessings of Christ in a life but even this small chapter is too much to believe. If the Gospel were not so fantastically good, more people would believe it! People do not reject Christ because He is not good enough but because He is too good to believe. What do each of you think of this viewpoint?
2. One of the blessings of Christ is joy. Someone has said: "Joy is the flag we fly from the castle-towers of our hearts when the Lord-King is in residence." Is there any truth to this in terms of your own experience? Please explain.
3. Look at the priorities listed on pages 132, 133. How does this square with your own experience?
4. Increasingly I feel:
   a. There is a single, simple problem: I-centeredness.
   b. There is a single, simple solution to life: surrender of the Self to God.
   c. There is a single, simple program: confession.
   d. There is a single, simple reward: a joyful freedom to be a human being.
   Let us react to these statements as personally as we are able.

Scripture Index

Genesis
1:27 13

II Samuel
22:28 62

II Kings
22:8 72

Psalms
8:5,6 14
103:3, 4 80

Ecclesiastes
12:13 30

Isaiah
17:9 38
24:5 62
53:6 38

Daniel
5:6 74
5:23 62

Zechariah
4:6 65

Matthew
3:2 23
4:17 23
9:2 82
9:22 59
10:39 52
12:45 109
16:19; 18:18 150

16:21, 22 36
16:23 36
16:25 102
18:20 126
20:16 102
25:40 109

Mark
8:12 59

Luke
4:18 87
4:18, 19 102
11:29 59
17:21 28
18:14 102

John
1:29 78
3:3 100
5:14 82
8:34 . . . . 84, 92, 105
8:36 . . . . 85, 89, 102
12:24, 25 102

Romans
1:19-2:5 23
2:15 78
3:20 . . . . 65, 77
3:28 65
6:3, 4 99
6:6, 7 24
7:7 77
7:18, 19 . . . . 85, 101
7:24 88

12:19 129
12:21 57
13:1 31
14:23 84

I Corinthians
1:27-31 100

Galatians
3:3 65
3:10 65

Ephesians
4:31 57

Colossians
1:20 128

Hebrews
4:12, 13 28

James
5:14, 16 82
5:16 150

I John
1:9 117
4:18 137

Subject Index

A

Adam 22
Alcoholics Anonymous 65
Alcoholics Anonymous 34,
  37, 42, 65, 68, 97, 98, 111, 120,
  137, 143-147
Alcoholism 34-36, 44, 45
American Medical Associa-
  tion 34
Anarchy of Feeling, The 15
Anger 135, 136
Appel, K. E. 56
Auricular Confession 111-114

B

Babson, Janis 15, 16
Battles, Ford Lewis 151
Belshazzar, King 74
Berne, Dr. Eric 38, 87
Beyond Ourselves 16
Bonhoeffer, Dietrich 113
Burns, Elizabeth 90, 91
Burns, Robert 27

C

Calvin, John 150, 151
Chronic worrier 63
Clark, David F. 104, 105
*Crisis in Psychiatry and
  Religion, The* 82, 96

D

Daniel 62
Discovering Ourselves 56

E

*Eighty-Eight Evangelistic
  Sermons* 114

Elliott, Lawrence 15

F

Faith at Work Magazine 103
Faith at Work movement 137
Fear 135, 136
Frank, Jerome 106
Frankl, Viktor 14, 16
Freud, Sigmund 15, 96
Freudianism 102

G

Gamblers Anonymous 137
Giles de la Tourette
  syndrome 104, 105
Gluttony 90
Gordon, S. D. 40
Guilt 80-83
Guilt and Grace 126, 128

H

Harris, Stanley 61
Heidelberg Catechism 95
Homicide 91
Hypochondriac 88

I

*Institutes of the Christian
  Religion* 151
Isaiah 38

J

Jeremiah 38
Josiah, King 72

K

koinonia 126

L

Larson, Bruce 133
Late Liz, The 91
Layman's Guide to Psychiatry
    and Psychoanalysis, A ...38, 87
Life Together 113
Little Girl's Gift, A 15
Living on the Growing
    Edge 133
Logotherapy and the
    Christian Faith 14

M

Man,
    Definition of 14-17
    Relationship to
        Divine Spirit 17
    Natural view of 24
    His egocentricity 27-39
    His anxiety 48
    His destructive urge ...56-60
    His resentment 56-58
    His feeling of
        omnipotence 63-67
    His feeling of
        omniscience 67-68
    His self-dependency ...68-69
    His bondage 84-92
Marshall, Catherine 16
McNeill, John T. 151
mea culpa 47
Meaning of Persons, The 14
Miller, Keith 40
Mowrer, O. Hobart 82, 96

N

Narcotics Anonymous 90, 137
Nebuchadnezzar, King 62
Neurasthenia 87
Neurotics Anonymous 137

P

Persuasion and Healing 106
Peter, Apostle 36
Prayer of confession 53

Q

Quiet Talks on Prayer 40

R

Raines, Robert 114
Reisman, David 122
Resentment 56-58
Reshaping the Christian
    Life 114

S

Schizophrenics Anonymous ..137
Schneiders, A. A. 15, 41
Search for Identity 76
Serenity Prayer, The ...42, 66, 67
Shoemaker, Samuel M. 114
Spinoza 7
Strecher, Edward A. 56

T

Taste of New Wine, The 40
Ten Commandments 73-76
Time Magazine 104
"To a Louse" 27
Tournier, Paul 14, 126, 128
Trevathan, Mary Margaret ...103
Tweedie, Donald F. 14
Twelve Steps and Twelve
    Traditions 65, 113, 148, 149

W

Wallis, Charles L. 114
Whitman, Charles 91